How to Survive Bereavement

How to Survive Bereavement

Andrea Kon

HELP YOURSELF

British Library Cataloguing in Publication Data
A record for this book is available from the British Library

ISBN 0 340 78624 8

Typeset by Avon Dataset Ltd, Bidford-on-Avon, Warks

Printed and bound in Great Britain by
Bookmarque

Hodder & Stoughton
A Division of Hodder Headline Ltd
338 Euston Road
London NW1 3BH

For Scott, Jamie and Sammy – who are the future

Contents

Foreword

'Death is nothing at all. I have only slipped away into the next room. I am I and you are you. Whatever we were to each other, that we are still.'

'All is Well', Henry Scott Holland

There are thousands of poems written for and by those who are grieving. This one – 'All is Well' penned by Henry Scott Holland, Canon of St Paul's Cathedral, nearly a century ago – has brought solace to millions. A copy was given to me just a few weeks after my adoptive mother and my beloved husband died within twelve hours of each other.

My mum's death had been expected. She had been so terribly ill that all the family prayed that her end would be swift and peaceful. My husband was with me when she died. When I cried on the way home from the hospital, he tried to comfort me by saying that no dog deserved to suffer the way she had been suffering. Yet, I loved this strong and courageous woman dearly. My birth mother had died when I was three years old and the stranger who'd married my father six months after her death took on the task of raising me, loving me, smacking me when I was naughty and, at other times, showing pride in me. She was the nearest person to a mother I knew. My father died three years before my mother and husband and so when I mourned, I mourned not just for mum but for a whole chapter of life, as most people do when their surviving parent dies. Suddenly, you are vulnerable. You are the next generation. That period of mourning was all too brief.

My husband died suddenly the following morning. It was totally unexpected. He hadn't been ill (as far as I was aware). He just had a heart attack and died. People told me that it must have been the shock of my mother's death that killed him, but that is not so. Clearly, he had been feeling unwell and had consulted our GP without my knowledge. He hadn't told me for fear of adding to my worries at what, he knew, was already a traumatic time.

It took me many years to come to terms with these two deaths and the circumstances that surrounded them. I tucked the poem 'All is Well' around the most recent photograph of my husband in the back of my organiser, and there it remains to this day, although I have remarried. The words are ingrained in my memory. I reread them whenever I feel particularly low or particularly high, sometimes at home, sometimes on the train to work. I read them whenever I wish I could share with my first husband both the large and small incidents which make up shared lives. As I read them, I feel myself reaching out to feel him, touch him, hear him, sense his remaining presence in my life and that of our two daughters and, now, the grandchildren he never knew.

Those who have endured bereavement know that death is not a subject many people want to talk about. Even those who have been bereaved tend to shy away from the very word 'death'. They use euphemisms such as 'passed away', 'passed on', 'departed' and 'gone' rather than mention the dreaded 'D' word. Yet death is something that affects us all, sooner or later.

When death strikes at the heart of a family, most people will pay homage to the memory of the departed, tolerate talk of the person and the event for a few weeks or possibly months, then they will tell those who mourn that it's time to 'let go'. What they don't understand is that it's not quite that simple: acknowledging the past while learning to live in the future is no easy task. My youngest daughter summed it up once by saying: 'There just comes a time when pain is no longer the boss.' And it's true. because the impossible does happen. You do learn to live and to laugh and find pleasure in life and in the world around you again. Each of us does it in our own way and in our own time, buoyed up by the support of family, friends and professional healers of mind and spirit. This book is intended as a practical guide not only for those who have been bereaved but for those around them who want to offer their help but don't know how.

My sincere thanks go to every single one of those kind people who agreed to talk openly and honestly to me about what is surely the most painful of all life events. My thanks, too, to the numerous organisations who gave their precious time to explain their work and who furnished me with essential literature.

I thank my editor, Judith Longman, who had such faith in me whenever I lacked confidence, and my agent, Fiona Lindsay at Limelight, who took me on and sorted me out. However, the biggest thanks of all go to Peter Gordon, my second husband, who encouraged me to write this book; supported me when the going got tough, helped me through the most difficult parts and who, most importantly of all, returned me to a life filled with love.

1

Living through bereavement

I remember the numbness I felt that first night, a Sunday night, when he was lying in the next room, looking for all the world as though he was asleep on the floor. Lying in the bath, I wondered why I didn't feel stressed and why I wasn't crying. I felt I ought to be – but I was someone else, looking in on this woman whose husband and mother had just died and who had no idea what to do about it all. It wasn't happening to me. This was something that happened to other people.

My daughters were in bed, exhausted after the events of a day which had no parallel in grief. The doctor gave them sedatives. I had sedatives too, but I didn't take them because I didn't think I needed them. Instead, I got our clothes, laying them out ready for the next day's funerals as if I were laying them out for school or work in the morning. It was July and muggily warm. I wondered whether we were going to be too hot in our long-sleeved blouses.

We observed our grief the Jewish way. We bury our dead quickly and on Monday morning the house filled with people. I just wanted them all to go away. It was a double funeral, first that of my mother, who had died less than twelve hours before my husband, and then that of my beloved Stanley. His sister was there, but I couldn't acknowledge her grief. My brother was there. He'd lost his mother,

1

but I couldn't acknowledge his loss either. My daughters were there. My poor girls: their world had crumbled, their darling daddy wasn't coming back and they only half believed it. The three of us stood with our arms around one another as the wooden box, with all the dreams of a joint future in it, was carried from the house. Someone tried to turn my face away but I wouldn't be moved. I had to see him go.

My mother had been in hospital, so her body would arrive at the cemetery separately. People whispered at me, 'How will you cope?' 'What will you do?' 'Will you move? Stay here? Work? Retire?', they kept asking if I was 'All right'. What could they do to help me? I wanted them to be quiet – yet I wanted to hear their voices because the last thing I really wanted was to be alone in the world. Suddenly, the buck stopped with me.

During the week of shiva (mourning) we sat on low stools – myself, my daughters, my husband's sister, my brother, my mother's sister and brother – and friends and relations came to pay their respects at the twice-daily prayers. The religious duties were performed correctly, although I knew my husband didn't really believe in all the ritual. Nevertheless, he'd done it for his parents and so I felt I had to do it for him.

In all the awfulness, there were moments of black humour. Someone has since told me that there are always moments of hilarity at times of grieving. My husband had a close friend who was at that time an MP and government Minister with a sensitive post which necessitated police protection. Naturally, with so many mourners, the house was filled with people, arriving with gifts of food and words of consolation, who came to offer us their condolences, sympathy and comfort. At 8 p.m. each night, the rabbi arrived and the house was literally bursting with bodies intent on attending the memorial prayers. On the night in question, among the comforters was this MP. An acquaintance came over to offer the traditional words of comfort: 'I wish you long life', but she was clearly over-emotional. Unable to contain herself at what she'd seen, she took my hand kindly – and then burst out with: 'I have been to many houses of mourning in my time. Do you know, there were so many people at prayers tonight that they were queuing down the path?' And then, clearly ready to broadcast the news to all and sundry next day, she informed me in an excited whisper: 'What a tribute to your mother and Stanley. It's unbelievable. I've never witnessed a policeman controlling the crowds at a shiva before.'

People kept saying: 'Be strong' because they didn't know what else to say. I told my sister-in-law that I had an answer for the next person who repeated those words. So when a relative stranger bid me 'Be strong', I replied, 'I know I've got to build up my strength, so I'm going to join a weightlifting class as soon as all this is over.' It was a stupid thing to say to a kind stranger – but in the aftermath of death, one does strange, irrational and often inexplicable things.

I remember the morning the shiva ended. The house was empty. The girls and I sat down to breakfast. None of us could eat. We were being sick by turns. I felt that putting food in my mouth was an act of disloyalty. How could I eat when he would never eat again? The girls, both in their late teens, wanted to be with their own friends and I understood that, yet I wanted them close all the time. They went out for a break and the house was so empty, as though its very heart had disappeared. I thought I wanted peace but I wanted noise. When they returned and made noise, I yearned for quiet.

There was so much to be done in the weeks that followed. Letters of condolence had to be answered and I was determined to reply to them all. The letters which meant most were the ones that recalled small personal details of Stanley, Mum or both of them. How, despite her illness and severe disability (she suffered from severe rheumatoid arthritis), Mum was a brilliant 'director of operations'. Her courage in the face of enormous pain. People remembered small things which Stanley had said and done with warmth. Some I knew of. Some I didn't. By acknowledging these acts of life, I felt both of them would live on in other people's memories as they did – and do – in mine.

When the numbness subsided, I began to perform the deeds which had to be done by rote. I had to make an appointment with our solicitor, which I did. I had to see the accountant. What accountant? My husband was the accountant. OK, ask solicitor! I needed to sort out bills. I did, and paid them. Luckily, I had always worked and had access to money that was mine. When someone dies, I soon discovered, joint assets are 'frozen'. I needed to apply for a widows' bereavement allowance. I wrote to the DSS. My younger daughter was about to start at university. I had to get her things together. This I did too. I had checklists of 'to do's' all around the house and I ticked them off merrily. Look everyone, I'm coping. I did what had to be done. Sometimes I did too much. I found a box full of old papers, some dating back six or seven years. I gave them a cursory glance. Figures and figures and yet more figures which meant nothing to me. I got hold of a big black plastic sack – and threw the whole lot away.

At first, I was scared to go out. I didn't want to meet familiar faces and have to explain what had happened. The first time I went shopping, I felt as though I was recovering from some dreadful illness. Whenever anyone asked me what was wrong with me, I'd burst into tears. I thought I was going mad. Other people have since told me they have felt exactly the same.

I'd cry on buses, the tube, or just in the street, for no reason. I hurt but there wasn't a pill that could take away the pain. When my caring GP offered me 'happy-drugs', I declined. I thought that Prozac, or one of its equivalents, would only mask problems, not cure them. So I carried on crying when I thought no one could see.

Everyone will tell you that grief comes in stages: first numbness and disbelief, then anger, then guilt at surviving, depression and sheer bloody pain. Unless you've experienced these emotions *in extremis* it's hard to describe them.

My anger developed around, of all things, a car. I know of other bereaved husbands and wives whose fury at the injustice of bereavement is triggered by anything from a bill in a restaurant that doesn't add up to the breaking of a mechanical object such as the washing machine. My anger crept up on me almost without me realising it, like an enormous rat, gnawing at my insides until suddenly I was empty of all but brute animal fury – at my husband for daring to die; at myself for being forced to survive; and at my family for somehow demanding of me that I carry on, like it or not. I think there are times when everyone who has been bereaved, particularly of a child or younger partner, feels suicidal. It all seems so unfair.

We had a beautiful company car. It was the car my husband had longed for and he had had it a mere six weeks at the time of his death. He was dead, yet the car sat resplendent in the garage, its red leather interior gleaming and still smelling the distinctive smell peculiar to new cars. And it had to be returned to the company.

We had a personalised numberplate (I have it still) which my husband had bought when he first passed his driving test and discovered that the Birmingham registration was KON. The car had to be taken to a registration office for the number to be transferred on to my vehicle (I certainly wasn't going to be 'robbed' of his numberplate, even if he had 'gone'), and my husband's boss asked me to drive it to South London. I was scared enough of the damn car during my husband's lifetime, in his death, I was petrified, so I refused. This meant it had to be collected by a fellow-director of the company. In retrospect, I realise they were all devastated by his sudden death.

Almost as soon as the formal period of mourning had ended, I decided to go back to work, to a job I had been about to embark on before my husband's death. Some people find work unthinkable after bereavement. For me, it was cathartic, the only part of my life that hadn't changed. My girls needed to get back to university and to 'normal' life, and although both had offered to stay with me in London, I told them – and meant it – that they needed to be where their father expected them to be. He was so proud of his girls' academic success and for me to have asked them to stay would have been downright cruel.

Thus, each night, I returned home to an empty house for the first time in my entire life, and every night the car was still there: I looked in the garage at 'his' car. I would open the door. Sit in it. Run my hands over the steering wheel. Remember the excitement of driving along in this lovely, white, gleaming dream automobile. Then

I would sob and scream and sob some more because the car was something else that had to go. Another part of my life that was only transitory. And because I refused to drive it, the company directors kept changing the arrangements for taking it away and re-registering the number.

On three occasions, arrangements to collect the car at a time convenient to me were aborted at the last minute. Each time, it became harder to think of parting with it. It took on a personality. I was growing 'close' to a machine. I felt I was parting with a bit of myself. When, finally, it was collected, I remember hurling a torrent of abuse at the poor, innocent man who arrived to drive it away. He must have thought me a wild creature and believed my husband well out of the way of such a vitriolic shrew. My daughters insisted it was 'only a car'. The point is that it was *his* car and I had no say over its future as I now apparently had no say over my own. The world was spinning round my head while I sat unmoving, in the centre of the typhoon.

I had to look for papers, sort out figures, deal with numbers. And the papers, oh, those papers, were the bane of my life. As I said before, I remember sitting on the floor in a bedroom, surrounded by papers I didn't understand, that were covered in figures which could have been double-Dutch for all I cared. I picked up the telephone, dialled his office number and, when the telephonist answered, asked for Mr Kon. There was an intake of breath at her end and, before she could reply, a shudder of horror at mine at what I had done. I slung down the phone and put all the papers into a big black plastic bag which I dumped by the dustbin. To this day, I have no idea what I threw away – but it cost me a great deal as the accountants fought to fill in the gaps and sort out the mess I had unwittingly created. The lesson I learned was that, no matter what the temptation, one should never, EVER throw anything away until one is absolutely sure it will never be needed again. I cover all this in the next chapter, but I'll risk being a bore by repeating it. It costs much less in both emotional and material terms to have professionals sort it all out than to have to trace, replicate and recover vital paperwork later on.

I was SO angry at my poor husband by this time. Angry at what I felt was his betrayal. How dare he abandon me, leave me, disappear when there were all these things to sort out – all these papers with figures on them to be attended to. We had shared an in-joke for years that we had only married because he couldn't spell and I couldn't add up! Was I suddenly supposed to learn, now, when there was so much else to cope with? How could he do this to me when he'd always told me he loved me? He'd left me with all his problems to sort out, as sole parent to his daughters and the figures were the final insult.

There was more than anger, though. I felt so guilty. Guilty for surviving when he had died. Guilty for daring to laugh occasionally and even feel relatively happy for brief moments. I was depressed by my own state and my inability to 'make things come right'. I slept only fitfully, often waking during the night to 'hear' his voice. I had nightmares in which a greasy figure of a man with a loud-checked jacket would break into my bedroom, stand over the bed and threaten me with – what, I don't know. I remember being too paralysed with fear to scream and I always woke in a sweat before he could spell out what he wanted of me.

I wanted physical contact, but if any friend's husband tried to kiss me in the friendly, platonic way he'd always done, I shuddered. I wanted the physical touch of only one man and that was beyond mortal grasp. When, on a train, I saw a bald-headed man, his pate dappled with freckles, I wanted to rush up and throw my arms round him and tell him the joke was over! I'd been punished enough. Strangers on the Northern Line tube must have been puzzled at the woman who would stand strap-hanging with tears dripping silently down her face.

I wanted my friends to treat me in the old, familiar way but they couldn't, and it irritated me. I could see their 'puppy dog' eyes of sadness when they looked at me, and I didn't want their pity. When they told me they 'understood' my pain, my desperate fight to be totally independent, and stopped talking to me about the annoying parts of their lives, apologising if they mentioned they were frustrated at the breakdown of a car or washing machine or irritated at their husband's strewing dirty socks around the bedroom, because they 'shouldn't moan about such things' to me, I wondered if I'd become an out-of-space alien. My friends didn't, couldn't, understand. I didn't ever want them to. I wanted them to stay my friends, however, and most, thankfully, did and still are – which I will deal with at greater length in Chapter 8.

I tried to look smart, as I've always attempted to look, so I made up every morning and people told me I 'looked wonderful'. I knew that behind my back they were saying I was 'doing well'. I could even hear my own voice criticising the new 'me', the freshly widowed woman who refused to wear widow's weeds; the 'Merry Widow'. This image grated because I was very far from being a 'merry widow' yet my mother had taught me that if you laugh, the world laughs with you, but when you cry, you cry alone. I felt I couldn't let my daughters see me breaking up inside because I felt that would be letting them down. I wish I had been more honest with them and more open to their needs.

Six months down the line, my girls were at university and seemingly 'settled', although I know now that this was far from the case. I was learning to live alone and loathed every second. I kept feeling that had it not been for work, which was the only part of my life which remained a constant, I would go mad. It even crossed my mind that if my husband could 'get out of it' I could too. It wouldn't be difficult to take a few pills too many. But then, what about our girls? Both rang daily to ensure I was coping. Sometimes they rang more than once. I thought I had fooled them into thinking all was well. I know better now. Both were totally devastated by all that had happened. I realised that succumbing to the temptation to 'end it all' was a coward's way out, or perhaps I was just too much of a coward to try!

One Friday night I came home and, to my despair, discovered a cherished cyclamen plant my husband had bought me was wilting. It was the final straw. It needed tending and I wasn't going to tend it. I screamed at it. 'Don't YOU dare die on me, you idiot piece of vegetation' and went to bed. When I got up next morning, it was standing bolt upright. It was as though there *was* something still alive that would listen to me.

On Saturday morning a friend dropped in as I was tending my plant and apologising profusely to its poor, frail leaves and feeling as though I must, truly, be going mad. I had to be the wildest, most unreasonable, stupidest woman in the world to be so angry and jealous of a man who had died through no fault of his own. He was the one missing out on his daughters, his life and the sun, shining outside in the now wintery, frost-spangled garden.

My friend had brought me a woman's magazine. 'I thought you might be interested in reading this,' she said, opening the magazine on the kitchen table and pointing to an article she had marked out with a yellow post-it. It was written by a woman who, like me, had lost her husband. She wrote about her feelings, the numbness, anger and despair, the unfairness of it all. She told of her unnatural reactions to normal things, of her attempts to re-build a 'new normality' and a life quite different from the life she had lived before. She said she had thought she was the only person to experience these emotions. She wrote that she thought she was losing her mind. That was exactly how I felt.

Until this point, I had spurned all thought of professional help. Me. The journalist. The one who wrote about other people with problems. I didn't need help, I was independent and quite capable of coping alone.

Suddenly, I realised that I needed help just like everyone else – and, having made that decision, I wanted it NOW. At the bottom of the article was a telephone number for CRUSE bereavement counselling. Before I had time to think about what I was doing, I dialled the number, half expecting to be patronised. Instead, the woman's voice on the end of the phone was kind and caring. I explained what had happened in a matter-of-fact manner. 'I'll have a counsellor contact you shortly,' she told me. And she did. The phone rang within ten minutes.

Jackie came to see me later that morning. When we began to talk, I wondered what good it would do. I could only tell her things from my current perspective. She is a clever woman and she could read between lines. She got beneath my skin to the soul of the relationships I'd had with both my mother and my husband and helped me understand that although their influence will always be with me, it was time to move forward. The whole process was hard work. I had counselling for eighteen months and it's something for which I will always be grateful. The counselling was entirely free. CRUSE do not ask for payment, but welcome donations if and when you are able to make them. They can be contacted at CRUSE House, 126 Sheen Road, Richmond, Surrey TW9 1UR. Their telephone number is 020 8939 9530, and their website is www. crusebereavementcare.org.uk.

I write of my own experiences in the context of this book only because I now know that mine were entirely normal reactions, although at the time, I felt like a freak. I have many friends who are or have been widows or widowers. Some, like me, lost their husbands or wives suddenly and without warning. Some lost their partners after long and lingering illnesses. One lost a sick child within months of losing her partner. The husbands of two of my girlfriends committed suicide. Each of us deals with death in a different way and the one thing I learned was that there is no 'right' way and no 'wrong' way of coping with bereavement.

People in middle age who lose parents often feel they can compare such a loss with that of losing a partner. From a personal perspective, they need to look again. Again from experience, and no matter whether the parent is reasonably young or respectably old, the loss is different. What most are mourning is the death not only of someone much loved, but of someone who stood in a generation between themselves and their own mortality. They become more vulnerable as a result of their loss. They have lost part of themselves.

When one loses a parent, that is the natural order of things. Losing a partner is sad – the cutting off of one half of oneself. It is possible, though, to grow and learn to 'stand on your own two little flat feet' as Jackie taught me, and survive. After all, the day you marry, you know that, barring accident, one of you must go first though you pray it will be later rather than sooner.

To lose a child is beyond my comprehension. I cannot understand how people are able to go on after losing a person whom they have created, who is proof of the continuum. It is against the natural order of things. But parents do survive and in another chapter I will be talking to some who came through and who managed to learn to smile again.

Whether to keep things or throw them away is a major decision. I kept letters of condolence for many years, hidden at the back of a drawer. At first, they bought me great comfort. Later, I found it hard to look at them. When I moved house, a friend who was helping me 'clear the decks' suggested I should throw away these letters. She was very 'tactful' with her suggestion. 'Of course, they're yours, but if you're making a new life, why hang on to the past?' was the gist of her message to me. At that time, I was open to all suggestions of ways to 'move forward' and I discarded them, keeping just one from a business colleague because it said so much about my husband. I lived to regret it – and I learned a bitter lesson: to do only the things I wanted to do and not what other people suggested might actually be 'good' for me. If you're a well-meaning friend in a 'suggestive' mood, bite your tongue. The only person who can be sure what's best for a grieving person is the person themselves.

For some people, as for me, the initial solution to loneliness was to work every hour of the day (and sometimes night). I had to keep busy. Others never want to work again. Every loss is individual and age, sex or status has no bearing on the suffering it causes. Those who have been in an unhappy partnership may be more inconsolable than those who have had a good relationship. There can be anger at the relief death finally brings, the words and the works left unsaid and undone. Life does go on, though, in an unremitting circle and as I discovered, you have to give yourself permission to re-enter the living world.

2

Nuts and bolts

The practicalities

When someone you love dies, the initial feeling is one of disbelief. It hasn't happened. He or she is coming back. 'I'm living in a nightmare and I'll wake up and find this isn't real.' Even when death has been expected, the finality of it all comes as a terrible shock. Sadly, it is all too real. Other people may be talking around your head (as they did round mine – *à la* 'Does he take sugar?'). If you have never had to deal with death before, the administration involved may appear over-whelming. Perhaps the worst time comes when someone asks you what you want done next – and you simply have no idea!

There are a series of essential official matters that must be seen to within hours of death. No doubt, you will be advised of these by the doctors who attend to certify the death, by funeral directors and other officialdom involved. They include:

- Registering death and obtaining a death certificate (which must be done within five days of death).
- Establishing cause.
- Notification of organ donation if that is your wish or the wish of the deceased.

- Tracing a will.
- Contacting funeral directors and making arrangements for the safe-keeping of the body until it is buried or cremated.
- Establishing any last wishes of the deceased regarding burial.
- Notifying official bodies such as banks and building societies that accounts need to be frozen. Informing social services if there are pensions involved.
- Establishing that any property is secured (particularly when the person who died lived alone).
- NB No property belonging to the deceased should be taken or disposed of in any way, no matter if you know it has been left to you, until *after* the grant of probate.

Organ donation

Most people who want to donate organs carry a card at all times, agreeing that in the event of their sudden death, their organs may be used for transplantation. The heart, kidneys, lungs, liver, pancreas, bowel or cornea may all offer life – or a better quality of life – to someone who is desperately sick. However, even a card-carrying potential donor's organs cannot be used to help give somebody that chance without the permission of the donor's next of kin. As the majority of human organs may need to be removed very rapidly – within half an hour of death – to be of any use (corneas need to be removed within twelve hours of death) it is vital that close friends and relatives are aware of the wishes of a donor, long before any other details concerning the death are dealt with.

Many people withhold permission for transplantation because they fear that there may still be the vestiges of life left while someone is on a life-support machine, or because they fear their loved one might suffer pain while the procedure is carried out. Be reassured that such fears are unfounded. A medical certificate certifying brain death must be issued by two doctors before any part of the body can be removed for transplantation.

Further information about carrying a donor card and the whole process of organ donation can be obtained at your doctor's surgery, at your health centre and at the Post Office. For further information about organ donation in Britain, you could contact the British Organ Donor Society, Balsham, Cambridge CB1 6DL. Telephone them on 01223 893 636 for further information, preferably faxing them first to make them aware that you will be calling. Alternatively, visit the Addenbrooke's hospital website at www.cambridge transplant.org.uk/index.html.

Wills

Everyone should make a will, regardless of their personal status. We all leave 'estates' (which despite their grand-sounding name may consist only of a toothbrush and a pair of pyjamas), but the bottom line is that although there is no inheritance tax to pay between a husband and wife, belongings of the deceased will need to be valued for probate.

A will can be lodged with a solicitor or at the Probate Registry, or in a bank or may simply be left in the keeping of a relative or friend. Someone close to the family should know where it is. If it is in the safe keeping of a solicitor or accountant it may be as well to ask them to look through it to check whether there are any specific instructions which need urgent attention. This is not so much that 'vulture' beneficiaries can swoop on the estate (they cannot and should not touch *anything* until after probate has been granted and this complex subject is dealt with a little further on), but is in case it contains specific details of how the deceased wants to be buried. They may have specified in a will whether they want to be buried or cremated, who they want to carry out the funeral service and even the clothes they wish to be buried in. This is not macabre but totally practical. If there is no will, the person is said to have died intestate, but more of that in a moment, too.

If someone is very sick and you know they are dying, it may seem insensitive to ask them where their will is. It needs to be done, however, if those nearest and dearest don't know. Making a deathbed will may sound Victorian and somewhat romantic, but not if you are the person who has to encourage someone who is dying to do just that to prevent major problems later. It is a very difficult thing to do because you are reinforcing and bringing into their focus the fact that they are dying, so if you, reading this, have not yet made a will, do it – for everyone's sake!

Executors

Executors are people selected by the person who has made the will to ensure that their wishes are followed as closely as possible. If it is a very old will and beneficiaries have since died, or their status has changed, executors have discretion to alter the will according to a change in circumstances. They are nominally responsible for ensuring that officialdom is notified of the death, that debts are paid, monies due to the estate gathered in and the profit and personal possessions distributed in accordance with the deceased's wishes. In practical terms, much of this can be handled on behalf of the executors by solicitors and accountants.

Dying intestate

When someone dies intestate, i.e. without leaving a will, the procedures to be followed are not only cumbersome and burdensome for those left behind grieving, but, at a time when the family does not need further hassle, they may also cause major disputes. This is a time when a family probably needs to pull together as a single unit more than at any other. The Probate Registry issues strict guidelines on the way the estate of a person who dies without leaving a will must be distributed – and it is important to note that cohabitees, no matter what the status of their dependence on the deceased, have *no rights at all in law.*

Cohabitees

In a world where it is common for people to live together as man and wife without the benefit of a marriage certificate, it is important to realise that cohabitees are entitled to nothing at present, as the law stands, regardless of whether they have lived together for eight days or 80 years, of who has kept whom, or whether the assets left by the deceased can be proved to have resulted as a result of the work of the pair as a partnership or couple. Cohabitees include any relationship where people are living together but are not married by a recognised religious or civil authority, and this includes gay and lesbian relationships. The new London Partnership Register being operated by the Greater London Authority for gays and lesbians, as well as for couples who want to formalise their relationship without a marriage ceremony, currently has no legal standing in Britain although the GLA are hoping that the Register will be the first step towards legalising partnerships for purposes such as wills, property and succession rights. Currently, though, no matter how committed the couple are, the law still regards them as cohabitees.

As a solicitor who specialises in estate administration explains: 'Cohabitees are in a very vulnerable position if someone dies without leaving a will. Under the laws of intestacy, which are very complex, they are not considered as beneficiaries, even if there is no living family and even if they were totally dependent upon the person who has died. If there are no children from the relationship, the estate will go to the deceased's parents, siblings or distant relatives. There is an immovable list of the way such an estate must be distributed.'

However, and unfair though it sounds, if you have a joint bank account, and it is in overdraft, responsibility for that overdraft will be the responsibility of the living cohabitee. The flip side of the coin is that any assets in that account will be yours. The message here is: if you are living with someone you care about and you wish them to inherit any or all of your estate, marry them and/or make a will. If you are gay, it is essential to make a will in order to ensure your loved one's inheritance.

Establishing cause

If the death occurs in hospital in England, Scotland or Wales, the body will be kept in the hospital mortuary until the next of kin arranges for it to be moved, either home or to a funeral parlour. If death occurs at home, you will have needed to call your doctor who will give you a medical certificate in a sealed envelope stating the cause of death. She or he will also give you a formal notice telling you how to get the death registered. Only after the doctor's visit can you call a funeral director to remove the body – this can be done immediately, or the body can be prepared for burial where it is, where religious rituals may be observed and where it will be left until the funeral.

If death is sudden, happens away from home, is suspicious, or if the dead person has not been seen by his or her doctor for more than two weeks, then the body may be taken to hospital for a post-mortem to establish the cause of death. There is no choice where a post-mortem is concerned: if cause of death is unknown, no matter what you believe to be the cause of death, it has to be done. You cannot refuse to permit it no matter how much you hate the idea. If the coroner carrying out the post-mortem finds that death was due to natural causes, they may issue the appropriate paperwork. Either the doctor or the coroner can sign the appropriate form if the body is to be cremated. Post-mortem should not delay a funeral unless there are suspicious circumstances.

Registering the death

In the UK, death must be registered within five days by the Registrar of Births and Deaths for the area in which the death occurred. Anyone registering a death will need to check when the Registrar's office is open and who needs to attend (it can vary from area to area). You will need to take some essential documentation and this includes:

- The medical certificate.
- The deceased's medical NHS card (if available).
- The essential 'pink paper' which will be issued by a coroner's office if the body is to be cremated.
- Details to prove the deceased's date and place of birth (a birth certificate or passport are usually the easiest way of proving this).

It will be necessary to list the deceased's occupation, full name, date of birth of a surviving spouse and whether the person who died was in receipt of a pension or benefit allowance from public funds. The informant will be given a document permitting them to arrange a cremation or burial, and a Certificate of Registration of Death (to be filled in if applicable).

You will need to pay for the death certificate and you will need extra copies for the estate to be administered, to pursue pension claims, insurance policies, savings bank certificates, shares and premium bonds.

Where the death certificate is necessary for official purposes, photocopies are not acceptable, so it will be cheaper and more sensible to pay for multiple copies at this stage – the price increases if you pay later. It may sound excessive but you will probably need about ten copies (and maybe more) which will be sent to banks, building societies, insurance companies, investment organisations, pension offices etc.

You can, of course, manage with just one or two copies, but as you will have to supply originals, this may mean waiting for someone to send you back the certificate before you can send it on to someone else, a slow and laborious business which can delay grant of probate and distribution and finalising the estate for many months.

Urgent practicalities

There are a number of practical matters which need to be attended to within days of the death, and even before the funeral in most cases. These include:

- Check the deceased person's diary for any hospital or dental appointments or important meetings and cancel them. Ensure that the deceased's home is secure if they lived alone, and stop deliveries of milk, papers and so on if other people who live in the house plan to stay with relatives during the period between the death and the funeral.

- Stop payments of direct debits, standing orders and relevant incoming payments where applicable. It may be necessary to change payments of essential services such as gas, electricity, water, telephone, TV licence and council tax into the name of surviving husband/wife or children if they are to continue living at the same address, even temporarily.
- Send copies of the death certificate to banks where the deceased held accounts so that these accounts can be frozen.
- If the house belonged to parents or someone living alone, make sure that the insurance is continued. Insurance cover stops on the death of the policyholder and will need to be reissued in another name. If the house is unoccupied, turn off the water and gas in summer – or make sure that the heating remains on at a low level in winter to prevent pipes bursting – and do check the property regularly.
- Bank accounts held in the name of the deceased person need to be frozen as soon as possible, especially if they are in overdraft, because otherwise interest on any loans will simply mount at what may suddenly appear an alarming rate. Specify to the banks that you would be grateful if they could freeze interest on the account. As debts as well as assets are only sorted after probate has been granted, and from the estate, this is a vital issue and, as already said, you will need to send the banks copies of the death certificate.
- Contact any companies with whom the deceased had credit, hire purchase or rental agreements for the same reason. Again, you will need to send copies of the death certificate.
- Inform the National Savings office if the dead person held any National Savings certificates or premium bonds (again, you will need copies of the death certificate).
- Payment of all bills, including utilities bills, accrued in the name of the person who has died will likewise need to be frozen. Again, you will need copies of the death certificate to prove the death. However, if you want supplies of gas, electricity, water and the telephone to continue, you will need to indicate this to the operating body at the time you notify them of the death – and

from thenceforth the person named on the bill will be responsible for its payment. If a property is to go into an 'estate' to be sold, it may be that the person paying the bills will need to reclaim the money from the estate at a later date – so do keep the bills and any other expenses incurred on behalf of the estate carefully.

- Notify social services if the dead person was in receipt of a pension of any kind, or any child benefit – they will also require copies of the death certificate.
- Notify private health insurance companies (who will often refund the unused proportion of a paid subscription).
- Notify any insurance or pension companies of the death. Yet again, a copy of the death certificate will be needed.

These may sound fairly obvious things to do, but in the heat of the traumatic moment, one or more can so easily be overlooked and may later cause all sorts of unnecessary hassle.

Burial or cremation

You will need to contact whoever holds a copy of the will (probably the solicitor or a bank) very quickly to discover whether the person who has died has left any specific requests for burial or cremation. If there is no will, the decision on what form the burial and service will take rests on the next of kin.

If the dead person was a Christian and lived or died in the parish of an Anglican church with space available in the churchyard, then he or she has the right to be buried in that graveyard. Most other religious denominations have their own burial grounds and their own ceremonies (see Chapter 4). Jewish people, for example, will almost certainly have paid for burial rights in a Jewish cemetery affiliated to their own synagogue as part of their synagogue membership.

Bodies may be buried in places other than cemeteries, including the sea (a special licence is required from the Ministry of Agriculture, Fisheries and Food and only about twenty such ceremonies take place annually because it is an extremely complex event to arrange.

Burials at sea can take place in just three locations – the Isle of Wight, Newquay and North Shields). People can also be buried in certain nature and woodland reserves (where burials cost around £600), or even in your own garden if you choose. This is amazingly simple, although it may be necessary to consult your local authority about environmental health issues. Estate agents advise that consideration be given to the impact a grave in the garden may have on the value of a property. You can contact organisations such as The Natural Death Centre and Green Undertakings for further guidance.

A funeral director will help answer questions and assist with arrangements including:

- Finding someone to help conduct the funeral in a manner befitting the wishes of the deceased or the next of kin.
- Arranging a 'viewing' to enable friends and relatives to pay their last respects.
- Providing the hearse and limousines.
- Choosing secular music or hymns to be played at the funeral.
- The floral tributes or charity donations.
- Newspaper announcements.
- Printed sheets of the order of service.
- Recording who attended (it is so easy for mourners to recall who *didn't* come, but so hard to remember who did).

The British Humanist Society can advise on non-religious ceremonies and has a large number of officiants able to perform most moving services which are entirely areligious.

Contacting a professional funeral director will remove much of the worry. These people are trained in organising a funeral just the way the dead person or their relatives want it, often not just the service itself but flowers, charity donations, placing notices or obituaries in the local papers, right down to arranging the wake or a small social gathering for the mourners following the religious ceremonies.

If the body is to be removed from a hospital, it is the funeral directors who will arrange for it to be laid to rest in a dignified place until the funeral, or who can arrange for the deceased to be laid out at home or in a church. They will ensure that if you wish to see your loved one once they have been prepared for burial, you can do so in a dignified and respectful manner. Many people find it a great comfort to bring along a gift or place letters, photographs or even garden flowers in the coffin and a good funeral director will make you aware of what you can do and how and when you can do it.

When you choose a funeral director, check whether he is a member of The Funeral Standards Council, the trade association of funeral directors, which regulates the professionalism of the services you will be offered. Funeral directors who are members will not only advise you on all the options available to you, including the place of burial or cremation, the preparation of the body and the kind of religious and non-religious services available to you, but may also recommend officiants and even help with your selection of the type of memorial. They also offer pricing standards – very important when you are planning a funeral and at a time when you may find it hard to concentrate on the 'nitty-gritty' details. If you'd like a list of their members, The Funeral Standards Council can be contacted at 30 North Road, Cardiff CF10 3DY. Their telephone number is: 029 2038 2046.

Payment

The cost of funerals may vary from country to country, from funeral director to funeral director, and according to religious belief and need. A traditional funeral director will probably charge from £1,200 upwards for cremation and £2,040 for an average burial service, although it can be much less or much more. If the deceased didn't arrange to cover the cost of their own funeral, or has no insurance policy to cover the cost, don't despair. Although the person making arrangements for the burial may be responsible for the cost of the funeral, it is possible to reclaim these costs from the 'estate' through the administrator of the estate.

Although you should have informed banks or insurance companies of the death by this time and accounts in the sole name of the deceased should be frozen, you will still have access to any accounts held in joint names. Building societies, life assurance companies and solicitors handling probate may be happy to make a limited sum available if there is a need. If there are difficulties because no such monies are available, and the spouse is in receipt of income support, income-based Job Seeker's Allowance, housing benefit or council tax benefit, it may be possible in certain circumstances to get a grant from the Department of Social Security's Social Fund which gives cash to those on such benefits to pay for the funeral of a friend or relative. To find out more about this, it will be necessary to visit the local Benefits Agency and ask for help. If no one is able or willing to arrange and pay for a funeral, the local council, or sometimes the health authority, may do so, but only where the funeral has not already been arranged. If it has, the money can generally be reclaimed from the estate.

State bereavement payments and allowances

Since April 2001, all widows and widowers are entitled to receive a tax-free lump sum of £2,000 that will be paid directly into a bank or building society account as soon as the authorities are notified and providing the following conditions are met:

- Your late spouse met the NI contribution conditions, *or* his/her death was caused by their job.
- The spouse was not entitled to Retirement Pension when he or she died, *or* you were under the State pension age when your husband/wife died.

The bereavement benefit is *not* payable if you were divorced or were living with someone else of the opposite sex as husband and wife at the time of your spouse's death.

Bereavement Allowance

You are entitled to a taxable weekly benefit from fifty-two weeks after the death of a husband or wife, providing you are over forty-five years of age and meet the conditions laid down by the Ministry of Social Security. The Bereavement Allowance replaces the old widow's pension, although it will be paid on the same conditions and at the same rate as the old pension. The amount you receive depends on your age at the time your spouse died.

If you are over fifty-five when you are widowed, you are entitled to the full rate Bereavement Allowance.

If you are aged between forty-five and fifty-four, you will only be entitled to part of the full rate, pro rata. The amount is fixed at the date of your partner's death and, unfair though it may seem, it does not increase with your birthdays.

Unlike the former widow's pension, social security will not pay SERPS (State Earnings Related Pension).

You will only be eligible for the Bereavement Allowance if:

- Your late husband or wife met the NI contribution conditions *or* his or her death was caused by their job.
- If you were aged forty-five or over when your husband or wife died.
- If you are NOT entitled to a Widowed Parent's Allowance.

Widowed Parent's Allowance

This includes:

- A basic allowance for you.
- An allowance for each of your dependent children *and* additional pension (SERPS) if you qualify.

BUT you will only be able to claim this allowance if:

- Your late husband or wife met the NI contributions *or* his or her death was caused by their job AND you have a child for whom you are entitled to receive Child Benefit.

24

- You are pregnant and expecting your late husband's baby – and this includes anyone pregnant as a result of assisted conception or IVF, as long as they there were living with their husband immediately before or at the time of death.

State retirement pension and SERPS

When you become of pensionable age you can claim a State Retirement Pension. If you are in receipt of a Bereavement Allowance or Widowed Parent's Allowance, and you have not remarried, you can now inherit any SERPS to which your husband or wife would have been entitled. If you did not qualify for the full rate of Bereavement Allowance because of your age at the time your husband or wife died, you will not now qualify for the full rate of SERPS.

New rules

As from 6 October 2002, a new rule comes into force that may affect your entitlement to SERPS. Changes will see the maximum amount of SERPS that a widow or widower may inherit from their late partner reduce from 100 per cent to 50 per cent of the previous entitlement. However, *nobody* widowed before 6 October 2002 will be affected by the new rule and if your husband or wife is due to reach state pension age before 6 October 2002, you will receive up to 100 per cent of their SERPS entitlement when they die.

If your husband or wife is due to reach state pension age after 5 October 2002 but before 6 October 2010, you will receive a maximum of between 60 per cent and 90 per cent of their SERPS entitlement. The exact amount will depend on when, in this period, they reached State Pension age.

However, such things have a habit of changing and you should contact your local social security office and ask for the New Bereavements Benefit booklet to ensure you receive everything to which you are entitled.

Grant of probate in England, Scotland and Wales

As soon as possible after a death, it is generally up to the nearest relative to discover whether the person who has died has left a will and appointed executors to administer the estate. It is the executor's (or executors') job to act as the deceased person's personal representative and they are responsible for paying all the dead person's outstanding debts, taxes and expenses, including all funeral expenses. These payments have to be made before any bequests can be handed out.

If there is no will and therefore no appointed executor, it will be necessary to apply for Letters of Administration from the Probate Registry (details of your nearest Registry are in the phone book).

If the estate is very small, less than £5,000 for example, this is quite a simple matter. If someone dies intestate, leaving property or any other substantial assets, things can become very complicated, which is why making a will is so essential at any time in your life.

Inheritance tax (at the time of going to press) is levelled at 40 per cent on all estates valued at more than £234,000. This includes the value of any property and the only time this tax is not payable is when the entire estate is left to the spouse. To obtain a grant of probate, which gives the executor or administrator of an estate permission to pay the bills and deal with the estate, the executor or administrator needs to fill in application forms from the nearest Probate Registry and attend at least one interview. A grant of probate cannot be issued until all due tax and inheritance tax has been paid.

It will be up to the executor or administrator of the estate to gain a valuation for probate. Debts cannot be paid, assets distributed or property sold or dispersed until probate has been granted.

Warning

- *Don't 'give' anyone anything from the dead person's possessions as a 'keepsake', even if their entitlement to it has been specified in a will, until AFTER probate has been granted.*
- *Don't be coerced or tempted into starting to 'clear up' until probate has been granted.*
- *Don't throw any papers (or anything else away) until after probate has been granted – no matter how out-of-date they look. Replacing such items as share certificates or tracing old insurance policies or savings plan information can cost a fortune and if you act in haste, you may regret it later.*

The Probate Registry (you will find the address and telephone number of your local Probate Registry office listed in the telephone directory) will send you detailed guidance on how to complete form IHT from the Inland Revenue's Capital Taxes office, so that they can assess how much inheritance tax is due. This leaflet includes details on how to fill out essential documents. You may need to call in an estate agent to value a property at current prices; gain access to safes and safe deposit boxes; and arrange for specialists to value any collections of, for example, stamps, jewellery or antiques. You will need to declare total assets belonging to the person who has died (before taking off the funeral expenses and any debts), including their share of assets held with someone else, gifts of cash, or stocks and shares quoted on the Stock Exchange and made up to seven years *before* they died. There are a number of exceptions to this, including wedding gifts to children and grandchildren. You will need to read through the form carefully to see exactly what the estate is liable to pay.

Remember, if the total sum remaining in the estate amounts to more than £234,000, inheritance tax will be levelled at 40 per cent of everything over and above that sum (including the value of any property).

There is no inheritance tax to pay between husbands and wives in Great Britain. For all other beneficiaries, including children, unmarried partners, parents and siblings, inheritance tax may be payable.

When the assets have been gathered in and assessed and the debts and taxes have been paid, the estate can be distributed according to the will, or according to the rules of intestacy. These are quite complicated and are available from a solicitor.

Cash and specific legacies are distributed first. Estate accounts need to be prepared if no claims are made within prescribed periods and all the rest of the beneficiaries will need to approve them. Then the remaining assets can be split in accordance with the will and signed receipts obtained from the beneficiaries.

If you have a problem sorting out an estate, seek advice from a solicitor or from the Citizen's Advice Bureau. This need not be an expensive business and if the estate is small, it may not be worth paying for the service of a solicitor who may charge £150 an hour. However, if you feel you need a solicitor's help, you can obtain the names of solicitors who offer a fixed-fee interview in the Solicitor's Regional Directory which you can find in local libraries, at the Citizen's Advice Bureau, through the Law Society, or through the courts. The law differs slightly in Scotland where a local Citizen's Advice Bureau will offer guidance.

When you are granted Letters of Administration by the Probate Registry, it may be useful (and is certainly cheaper) to apply for several copies at the same time. Just as with the certificate of death, you will need to send original documents to insurance companies, banks, and whoever else may need to release funds for distribution, and in order to get permission to sell a property. Each copy costs £5 (at the time of going to press) for the first copy, and £1 for each subsequent copy issued at the same time. If you need to apply for further copies later, you will find the £5 charge clicks back into place again. Not only can a shortage of copies hold up the whole process, but it can prove extremely expensive in the long run.

After the essentials

In the effort to make sure that everything is done correctly, it is easy to overlook minor details which can cause a surprising amount of pain and reawaken raw wounds if they are not seen to fairly soon after death has occurred. These include:

- Returning passports to the Passport Office. They will return the passport to you with the corner removed and stamped 'cancelled' if you ask them to do so.
- Returning a driving licence.
- Returning library books, library tickets and hospital equipment such as hearing aids, wheelchairs or walking sticks.
- Claiming refunds on season tickets (you may need the Death Certificate here to ensure a refund is paid to the estate).
- Cancelling membership of clubs and associations.

It all sounds a lot to do when you already have so many emotions coursing round your head. But it can be done. Accept all the professional help you can get.

3

Coming to terms

'Coming to terms with' is an ambiguous phrase. How can you 'come to terms' with the death of someone you love so much? It doesn't take long to realise that when a loved one is missing from your life, nothing will ever be quite the same again. There's certainly no doubt that the deaths of around three and a half thousand people, murdered in September 2001 by the terrorists who destroyed the World Trade Centre on New York's Manhattan Island and who launched attacks on the Pentagon in Washington and Pennsylvania, changed the whole world for ever. Their deaths directly affected the way people talked to one another in public and in private. Even people indirectly affected by the catastrophic events of these terrorist attacks mourned for those who died.

What happened in the USA was, however, too enormous and too horrendous for us to comprehend at first. It was only as the personal stories started to filter through, of the new father whose baby was born just hours after his death in one of the planes; of the young mother who left her five-year-old and seven-year-old in her husband's care as she set off for a business meeting in New York; of Barbara Olsen, wife of US Solicitor General Theodore Olsen, who was a passenger on one of the planes which ploughed into the World Trade Centre; and of the Franciscan priest Fr Mychal Judge, chaplain to the New York City Fire Department, that it was possible to see this holocaust of innocents on an individual basis. For every member of every family who has lost a loved one, the simplest things change – things that no one thinks about, tells you about, or warns you to expect.

It takes a long time before a visit to the supermarket becomes a routine experience. You reach out for the cheese counter to buy your partner's favourite cheese, only to realise that they're not there to eat it. You may still be taking the same train to work, but the person who always dropped you at the station doesn't do so any more. You may burst into tears as you walk into a car-park, because a voice inside your head begins to ask: 'What would he/she have said if they could have seen me now, fighting to clear frost from the car windscreen? Or you find yourself arriving home to an empty house, so quiet, so cold, that the silence is tangible and ice freezes your heart, even in mid-summer. I admit that there is certainly a degree of self-pity involved. Whether the death is that of someone brave, someone young, someone much-beloved, someone old, someone beautiful in character, one feels pity for what seems like such a senseless, worthless, useless loss.

People are very good at offering advice, of course. I would be told that 'everyone' said I should sell my home, get a dog for company, change my car, go out, meet people, get counselling. My answer was: 'Introduce me to this "Mr or Mrs Everyone" and I'll tell them what I think of them.'

Where did they want me to move to and why? Why did death mean I also had to part with my home? Where should I go out to (it was mid-winter)? Was I expected to sit on a cold park bench when what I really wanted was to sit on my own settee in my own warm home. All such well-meaning advice on top of your own emotions can make life feel like an unbearable burden. The one thing you need to be certain of is that any major decisions you make are your own and not decisions 'everyone' thinks would be best for you.

Whether you have experienced death as a result of a long illness, sudden illness, terrorist attack, tragic accident or age, whether the person who died and those who are left behind are young or older, whether or not there is an initial feeling of release that death has finally ended much suffering, or whether there is the additional shock and horror of the unexpected to contend with, it hurts like hell.

You will experience denial – this has to be a nightmare, it can't be true – you will almost certainly go looking for your loved one in the street, or be convinced you spot them in a crowd. You will feel angry, guilty, depressed at times, and these feelings may merge and overlap. You may be frustrated at the helplessness of your situation, too. There are all the 'what ifs' and 'if onlys'.

Time-spans

Some well-intentioned books may tell you that there are time-spans to these emotions. I believe people who say such things are offering a false kindness – and Renee, who lost her seventeen-year-old son Paul nineteen years ago, agrees with me: 'I have been without Paul longer than I had him,' she says. 'Sometimes, even now, when I talk about him, the tears well up. People say: "I would have thought you'd be over it by now." But you never "get over it". You carry on living, but the person you have lost is always with you.'

I can tell you from experience that there is no time-span involved. Bereavement isn't a virulent disease which has a set recuperation period after which you will be 'all better'. There are no 'average' time-spans for the period of grieving, and what may affect one person will have no bearing on the way another reacts. Just as no two relationships are ever the same, so no two bereavements can ever be compared. Grief is individual. You can tell anyone who dares to suggest you should have 'got over it by now' that although you are living in the present and have moved on, they must know that you will love and remember whoever it is you have lost until the day you, too, die. You can say quite firmly that you haven't had a virus. You've had a death. There is nothing abnormal or unnatural in finding yourself in floods of tears, even years later, at a single significant life-event, such as a wedding or the birth of a new baby in the bereaved family. To me, that is the meaning of everlasting life. Even when we have died physically, we live on in the memories of those who have loved us.

If only . . .

All of us question our own actions at the time of death. 'If only I had called the ambulance sooner', 'If only I had realised how ill she/he looked' or 'If only I had said, done, been here, there, remembered . . .' and 'Did I do the right thing?' I remember going to see my own doctor after my first husband's death because I was convinced that if I hadn't been so wrapped up in my mother's illness, I might have noticed that he was unwell and then something preventative could have been done. The doctor reassured me that there was nothing I could have done to stop his death. However, it may take many years before you are able to believe something like this. I'm now a fatalist: after meeting many people who have suffered the agonies of bereavement and who have questioned themselves and everyone around them, I have come to believe very firmly that when your number is on the ticket, your time is up.

Clearing up

Perhaps one of the hardest ordeals anyone faces after death is 'clearing up'. We all have possessions, and, after someone has died, their things may take on an entirely different meaning. How quickly is it 'decent' to clear away what appear to be the last vestiges of someone else's life? When you discard or give away their possessions, are you discarding their souls?

In her book *You'll Get Over It*, Virginia Ironside writes:

The truth is that after death, things are no longer mere trinkets. Pieces of furniture are not bits of wood; money is not cash; houses are not bricks and mortar. The loved one has gone, so the possessions take on this mysterious meaning, as if they are the last link with the dead people, often becoming imbued with their very lost selves, talismen of their souls. There is a particular saucer that 'is' my mother. Whenever I look at it, she's there. If someone else were to take it, I would be furious and fight for it. To outsiders, it would seem as if I were squabbling over a cracked piece of china; I would actually be fighting for dear life for a part of her.

Clearing up and clearing away is an awful job. The longer you leave it, the harder it is. I gave my husband's clothes away to charity, which was the easy bit. I had cufflinks made into charms for my daughters so that each could wear one round her neck and think of her dad. Other items such as watches, I put away for the time when I would have sons-in-law and grandsons in the hope that they would appreciate something that once belonged to a beloved father. But, after my own double bereavement, I had the awful task of clearing out my parents' flat on my own. Unfortunately, my brother was unable to help as he was working abroad most of the time.

I remember taking everything out of the kitchen cupboards, piling it all in a huge heap on the floor and looking at the remnants of my own childhood. There was 'my' cheese plate, Dad's favourite knife, that awful plate that no one liked and no one wanted to throw away. There were gadgets never used (and never likely to be now), and the mincer my mum had used to puree my brother's food when he was a baby. I sat and howled.

I met a man who wasn't there

Many people feel that they are 'abnormal' when their whole lives appear to be dominated by someone who isn't there. They may get up in the morning and the person they want to say 'good morning' to is missing. There's no one to fight over for the bathroom. No one to complain that the tea's too hot or their eggs are too hard or too soft, no one to nag them for being late. They may find there's nothing to tidy because no one has made a mess, or be irritated with themselves for being messy when there's no one else to blame. They go to work and the routine of speaking to a loved one during the day is broken. There's no one to rush home to. No one to row with.

No one to touch or cuddle. The dead person becomes a 'missing link' between themselves and the old order of things – the normality that was. This is when it becomes essential to break old routines and find new ones.

When Aileen's husband died suddenly as the result of a tragic road accident, her teenage daughters reacted entirely differently. The older girl, then aged twenty, had rowed with her father the week before his death and had never seen him alive again, although they had made up on the phone. Bernice came home for the funeral, but gave no outward sign of mourning, insisting that life must go on and carrying on with her own social life as though nothing had happened to the amazed horror of her mother who felt alienated and couldn't believe what was happening. Had her daughter cared so little for her father that she could go out on her usual Saturday-night jaunt just two weeks after his death as though nothing had happened? Was her daughter, one so loving, now so insensitive to her mother's needs that she could carry on as normal?

Bernice began a relationship with a man Aileen knew her husband would have disliked intensely. He teased Bernice unmercifully, telling her she'd be beautiful if she wasn't so fat, that she'd be lovable if she looked after herself and then, just four months after her father's death, he dumped her. The diet on which Bernice had embarked became anorexia and bulimia. Her weight plummeted from more than eleven stone to just six-and-a-half. She was hospitalised. Aileen and her younger daughter, who had now bestowed upon herself the heavy mantle of 'carer' to both her mother and her sister, were called in to family therapy sessions. At this point, Aileen panicked. Her grief at losing her husband turned to fury at him for having 'left me in this shit'.

'It was four months down the line, but it felt as though it was all happening all over again,' she says. 'We were called in one day and we sat in front of my daughter and her therapist while Bernice threw every wicked line in the book at the pair of us. She ranted on about how her sister had attacked her with a carving knife. She told me I had been a wicked mother. I had hated all her friends since she'd been a little girl. I had beaten her and on one occasion I had laid her on the floor, sat on her, grabbed her ears and banged her head up and down on the floor by levering her head with her ears. It was like being in a horror movie. When we got outside, my younger daughter and I both sobbed. I couldn't drive for almost an hour. How could this be happening? How could he let it happen?' she says.

I can clearly remember feeling so furious with my husband for daring to die when I needed him, and for feeling so foolish at my anger because common sense told me that he knew he had so much more to do and see before he would have wanted his life to end. The guilt is not only guilt at feeling so stupid. It's also the guilt of being a survivor when someone you love has gone first.

Miriam and Anton

Miriam and Anton had been married for eight years when he died suddenly of a heart attack. Anton had adopted Miriam's daughter Rebecca as his own, and as Miriam mourned her husband, so her daughter mourned the only father she could remember.

'Apart from the horror of my husband not being there any more, I felt so scared. I didn't know what I was scared of. It was anything and everything. I had no idea of where I was going or what I was going to do. I remember sweeping snow from the front of my home that first winter in tears. Sweeping and sweeping it away, bawling my eyes out. My neighbour came and grabbed the shovel away from me and carried on for me. His wife took me back to her house for a cup of tea while he swept the path,' she told me.

Miriam says that for a long time after Anton's death, she continued to buy his favourite cakes and biscuits. 'The thing I avoided above all others was walking through any men's wear department,' she says. 'I would walk all the way round the outskirts of a shop like Marks & Spencer, rather than take the quick route through men's wear.

'I lived in a small village. I'd walk into the butcher's and they'd say, "How are you?" in that soft, caring sort of voice that brought me to tears. I wanted them to treat me normally, but, of course, I didn't feel "normal" and I didn't behave "normally". I used to walk out without buying anything because I couldn't talk for the tears that choked my throat.

'For ages, my mum did a lot of my shopping. I was a basket-case for a long while. I didn't go out at all. Because I needed someone to buy things for, I over-indulged my daughter who was then thirteen. I bought her loads of expensive foods that she specifically liked, clothes, CDs – just to have someone to focus on.'

It is the lack of focus that can make life seem so entirely pointless for a very long time. But there are ways to try to refocus your life. Perhaps the most important is to try to find others in a similar situation to yourself (no two situations are ever totally comparable or totally the same). Ask yourself: Do I know anyone else in a similar situation? Do any of my friends or colleagues know other people in a similar situation?

You might well be able to form a self-help group for people just like yourself. You could:

- Write a letter to your local paper explaining your predicament and asking whether anyone else out there would like to share your interests.
- Ask your doctor, social worker or bereavement counsellor if they are aware of any groups you could join specific to your needs.
- Surf the Web, using your particular problem as a keyword in a search engine such as Google, Yahoo or Alta Vista to see what else is available.

Miriam says she chose not to have bereavement counselling. 'I'm just one of those people who has to work through things in my own head,' she explains. 'I'm not one of those who can talk easily to strangers. I thought that no one else could do this for me. It was something I had to work through for myself.

'Dealing with Rebecca was a horrendous experience. Initially, she wouldn't eat, drink, or talk to anyone, including me. About midday, the day after Anton's death, a religious minister came to talk to both of us. He took her into her room and it was as though someone had turned a switch on in her head. She was back to normal again, except she wasn't normal. She was so angry. She wasn't only angry with me. She was angry with Anton, with herself, and with everything and everyone around her. She was angry with God as well. She wouldn't come to the funeral. She wouldn't worship with me. She gave up religion. She stayed that way for two horrible years.'

Miriam says that when her mother died seven years later, the loss was entirely different. 'For a start, it was expected. I remember thinking that this woman had known everything there was to know about me for forty-six years. I shared every part of my life with her and who was I going to share things with now. I was angry this time, mainly because of the way my stepfather behaved during the last two years of her life. It is a lot easier to be angry than to be hurt and upset. Anger removes much of the pain of the loss. The anger can become a place to focus instead of dwelling on the hurt. I felt that my wishes and those of my sister regarding our mother's final resting place were of no consequence to our stepfather and that soured my relationship with him. I have only visited him once since my mother's death.'

Siobhan and Matthew

Siobhan was sixty when her husband Matthew died. During their forty years of marriage, he had had numerous affairs. Each time, she took him back, but never quite forgave his unfaithfulness; the prospect of life alone was infinitely worse to her than his dalliances. During the last seven years of their marriage, he had been faithful and she had begun to relax for the first time – although she never missed an opportunity to remind him of how good she was to have resumed the relationship.

When he died unexpectedly at the age of sixty-two after a short illness, her grief knew no bounds. Finally, he had done what she had dreaded for all those years. He had left her all alone. Well provided for financially, she was the 'poor little rich girl' with a great deal of money, but no one to spend it with. Whenever and wherever she was, she moaned at her plight. She became a martyr to her own cause. 'I took him back and then look what happened,' was the cry constantly underlying her every word. At first she was frequently entertained and invited to people's homes but then the entertaining stopped because she never asked people back. When she finally sold the business she had run with her husband, she refused to take up voluntary work because it was beneath her. As their friends drifted, she moaned to those left to listen that 'no one wants me any more'. The final indignity came when she had a brief affair with her oldest friend's married brother. They were discovered, and despite the fact that they swore that it had not been a physical affair, no one truly believed it. Not surprisingly, the friend, a widow with whom she had been able to spend much of her time, became an ex-friend. Siobhan was now high and dry, spending much of her day in her dressing gown and trying to drown her sorrows in the whisky bottle. Her daughters were unable and, on many occasions, unwilling to help her. Today, the more she hits out verbally at those around her, the further away she pushes them and the lonelier she becomes.

Lashing out at people around you, whether verbally or physically (even if it is for reasons that neither you nor they can understand), is not the answer. But there is a desperate need to get rid of the pent-up energy that is the flip side of anger. It helps if you can find an outlet. I took up swimming. Interestingly, it was something Miriam did too. I used to go swimming every night. It was something I had never done before, but it was a way of releasing the pent up super-energy that haunted me.

It is easy to become belligerent. When your washing machine breaks down and you start shouting at the repairman who can't come for a week, he doesn't know it's not actually him you're fighting – but your own anger. You transfer the feelings of fury you feel against your dead partner for leaving you, and against yourself for feeling so stupid at being angry with someone who is dead, to anyone who crosses you, however mildly.

When anger, grief and despair threaten to overwhelm you, it can be helpful to take a stiff drink, sit quietly and make an honest list of all the things you are really angry about. Is it the washing machine that is bugging you, or the fact that you can't deal with it? Is it the failure of someone or something to behave how you want them to, or are you demanding too much? Can your energy be turned from the negative to the positive?

Peter and Alex

Peter was distraught and utterly devastated when his wife Alex died, after years battling with cancer. She had struggled for many years to set up her own home-made chocolate business, creating wonderful confections for love rather than money, and it was suddenly all beginning to come right. The year before she died, she was in remission and the business went into profit for the first time. She and Peter even started to talk about sending their son, Charlie, to a private school on her profits. Then she relapsed. Peter gave up his own job as a corporate accountant to nurse her through the last few painful months and care for Charlie. He arranged for Alex's assistant to take over the making of her confections.

'I didn't have a job, so I decided that I would learn how to make chocolates too and open the shop that was Alex's dream,' he says. 'Charlie found it was fun to come home from school and help me make chocolates. Once the novelty of eating more than he produced wore off we found it brought us closer together and afforded us a lot of fun.

'I called the little shop Queen Alexandra's in Alex's memory because she was the Queen of our family. So far, it has proved a great success – although some of my relatives tease me that with a name like that it has to be a covert name for a pub or bar. I found being busy was the answer. It has taken a long time to accept that Alex isn't going to walk in one day and tell me that I'm doing it all wrong! But I think that making her dream into a reality has given my life focus when I needed it most. Alex is still the centre of my world.'

In an interview with Sue Corrigan in *Night and Day*, the *Mail on Sunday* magazine, cellist Julian Lloyd Webber remarks:

At the beginning of the last century, the average life expectancy in the United States was about forty-two. Today, everyone in the

West is expecting to live to eighty or ninety. People in other parts of the world, such as Africa, are surrounded by death all the time, but we think we must stay alive at all costs.

He continues:

If someone dies aged sixty, it seems to be an absolute tragedy, whereas a hundred years ago, that was seen as a very ripe old age. There is a wonderful image in the Bible, in words written I think by St Paul, that the human body is just like a mist. You see it briefly, and then it's gone. And for me, that's a wonderful description because it puts everything in perspective. In my view, we should all take more notice of those words of St Paul. We all take ourselves far too seriously.

This is his view on dying, but learning to live without a loved one is not easy. Whether you have lost a parent, a partner or the greatest apparent injustice of all, a child, you need to go on living, as opposed to merely existing, for your own sake.

Judgements

You need also to be aware that you will be judged by others who have not the slightest inkling of your emotions. If you continue to dress well, wear or make-up clean, attractive clothes, people will tell you how 'well' you look when what they mean is: 'How could she/he?' If you walk around in dowdy tatters, you will be accused of 'letting yourself go'. You are in a damned-if-you-do and damned-if-you-don't situation.

Just ten days after my husband's death, I had to pay a visit to our family solicitor who was also a business colleague of my husband's. I remember doing my hair, putting on my 'face' and a cream-and-blue patterned dress which was the last thing my husband had bought me because I was going to this meeting as 'Stanley Kon's wife' and didn't want him to be ashamed of me. I didn't want the solicitor, who has since become a friend, to wonder what on earth my husband had 'seen in me'. I wanted to be dignified so that he would be proud of me wherever he was, looking as he had always liked me to look. On the platform waiting for the train, I bumped into an acquaintance who had heard what had happened. 'You look nice,' she said, unable to disguise the surprise in her voice. I murmured my thanks, and afterwards realised she had expected me to be dressed in widow's weeds. But I continued to dress and make an effort, to make up every day, because somewhere in the back of my mind was the sneaky suspicion that I might bump into my husband somewhere and discover it *was* all a horrible nightmare. Of course, I was what the psychologists call 'in denial' – but so what. The lesson I learned, once again, is: 'Behave how you feel comfortable behaving, whatever your private reasoning. Be comfortable with yourself.'

Death isn't catching

I know of lots of people who have caught colds. Yet I have never met anyone who has 'caught' death and 'passed' it on. Once the initial shock of a sudden death has receded in other people's minds, it is often replaced by the illogical belief that the death, particularly the death of a young person, has in some way 'tainted' the survivors and may even be 'catching'. It is as though when bad things happen, they are a variant of chicken pox.

This is not an unusual emotion. As my birth mother died when I was three years old, my darling dad when I was forty, and then my adoptive mum and my husband so soon after one another when I was forty-three (OK, so you've worked out how old I am!), I felt like 'bad news'. It didn't help when people looked at me with what I can only describe as spaniel puppy-dog eyes (large and so sad) and said: 'But you're so young', as though my age had some direct bearing on the events in my life. So when people asked about my family, I turned it into the manner of an Oscar Wilde joke and said I was 'a bit careless with my relatives. I seemed to lose an awful lot of them'.

In fact, for many years, I wouldn't have a relationship for fear that if I dared to love someone too much, they would go and die on me. It was, I admit now, rather presumptuous to assume such power, but it's a feeling many bereaved people share, particularly when a number of relatives have died in fairly fast succession.

Nigella Lawson, whose husband John Diamond died from cancer of the tongue and throat, recently described a similar feeling in newspaper interviews. 'Family members suffering from cancer avoid me because my mother, my sister and then my husband all died from cancer,' she told newspapers. 'It was as though contact with me would in some way make them more vulnerable to the disease of death,' she said.

Laurie and Roger, whose baby daughter Rebecca died suddenly from meningitis although she had been ill for all ten months of her little life, explain how although initially people were generally 'wonderful', their reactions later left them feeling socially excluded. Says Laurie: 'Immediately after the funeral we received an awful lot of attention. Once the attention went away, Elizabeth, our three-year-old, and I were almost like social lepers. People weren't sure whether to invite us to things or not – as though we might in some way remind them of their own family's frailty or their own vulnerability. The excuse they offered was that it might hurt me to see other women with their two children when I had just one left. When people ask me how many children I have, I reply "Two – but one died." That at least makes me feel "normal". I am not denying my daughter's existence.'

Even professionals, supposedly trained in the art of dealing with death and those who are in shock at a sudden death, are sometimes totally insensitive. 'After Rebecca's death, the police were called as they are at such times. I remember the policewoman trying to comfort us by telling us she knew just how we felt because her dog had died recently! I think she thought she was being empathetic,' says Laurie.

I know I had similar experiences. Within a week of my husband's death, someone said to me: 'Never mind, dear. You're young. You'll marry again.' I know people who have lost babies and young children and who have been told by well-meaning but utterly thoughtless friends: 'You're young. You can have another.' The simple fact is that no other person can ever replace the person who has died. Any future children grieving parents have will be their own people, not replacements.

When I did marry again, my new husband and I came to an agreement. We would both talk freely, openly and naturally about all the people we'd loved and lost, not in any forced way, but just as they appeared in and influenced our past lives: our parents; his partner; my husband . . . They helped to fashion us into the people we are now. To deny their existence would be to deny ourselves.

It's almost always up to the bereaved person to take the lead. If you can, tell just one close friend to act as your spokesperson. Let it be known that you are happy to speak your loved one's name as a matter of course, just as you've always spoken of them, and that you won't dissolve in a sea of salt-water tears.

Letting go

There are ways in which you can help yourself accept what is, let go of what was, and find a new 'normality', but first you need to look at the way in which you are thinking. Do you consistently:

- Think or say to others: 'If my loved one was here I would or wouldn't be doing this?'
- Listen to what you think they would have said before you make a decision?
- Choose to wear clothes they would have liked, even when they may not have been exactly what you preferred to wear?
- Go to places they would have enjoyed; chosen food or a drink in a restaurant they would have chosen?
- Said what you think they would have said rather than what you really wanted to say or mean?

If you have answered yes to more than two of the above (and all of us do all of these things at first as a matter of habit), you have a long way to go to acceptance. You are caught in a time-warp and you need to extricate yourself from the tangle of the past web of your life before you can move forward.

It's not an easy process. You are going to need to work at learning to stand alone as a separate, whole independent human being and it isn't easy. To start with, you need to look at yourself as an individual. If you have lost a parent, you need to learn to respect yourself as the adult you now are, even if you have long ago taken over the role of 'carer'. If it is a partner who has died, you need to reassemble the 'I' you were before you became part of 'we'.

Becoming half of a couple means moulding to, around and even into the personae of the person to whom you are attached. Now you need to separate the Siamese element of yourself. When you're talking to friends as half of a pair, it's perfectly normal to say: 'We love eating at a particular restaurant', 'We love the theatre, particularly musicals', or 'We really don't enjoy hot-metal concerts.' The 'we' may not, but what does the 'I' really like?

It can be a journey of self-discovery. Learning to accept a situation you don't want to be in isn't fun – but discovering yourself and your individual likes and dislikes again can be.

- List five things you planned to do before you teamed up, and set in motion ways in which you might be able to achieve at least two of them.
- Treat yourself if there's no one to do it for you. It may be as simple as buying your favourite ice-cream or a bunch of flowers. Or just laying in a warm bath with a drink and a book or a couple of cold tea bags to freshen tired, sore eyes.
- Plan an outing with a friend you really like, perhaps someone your partner never got on with – or search for a friend with whom you've lost touch.
- Did you once have a hobby you dropped when you became half of a couple? Could you pick it up again?

Closing the circle

You cannot begin to go forward until you yourself find a way of 'closing the circle' of life with someone. It may mean paying a visit to a place you both loved, or of finding the courage to enjoy a piece of music that was 'your song'. You may need to go on a journey to finish unfinished business.

Perhaps it's because I'm a writer by nature, but I found writing very therapeutic. Soon after my husband died, once the girls had gone off to university, I went to stay with some relatives abroad for a week. While they were at work, I would go to the beach or the park and sit for hours writing long letters to my husband, as if I'd just left him at home. I managed to tell him all the things I didn't have a chance to say before he died. I told him how much I loved him, I told him what his daughters were doing; what I was doing; what I was thinking, I even wrote how angry I was with him for dying and how sorry I was that he was missing out.

I really felt he was receiving those words. I tucked the letters away and went for a walk on a beach we had often walked on together and collected shells, just as we used to. I went back to the hotel where we had spent our last holiday and ate an ice-cream he loved (even though I didn't like it at all). I closed our circle. All the love remains there and I felt, and feel, better for having done it.

Your circle may be something entirely different. Think about it. What were your best times together? What were the worst? Be honest with yourself. If you can find your own way to 'close your circle', sitting by a grave, walking alone or writing a letter or diary, it will help you to find a place from where you can start building all over again.

This time last year

Most of us who have suffered the loss of someone close know the 'this time last . . .' syndrome. It may start as 'this time yesterday we were . . .' Then become 'this time last week . . . this time last month . . . this time last year.' It is true to say that the first anniversaries are the hardest of all: the first birthdays without, the first Christmas without, the first wedding anniversary without. They are all major events that you had hoped would be memorable and are now memorable for all the wrong reasons.

There is no magic cure I can offer for overcoming these times. You can't run away from them no matter how hard you try. At the time of my husband's death, we had been planning our silver wedding celebrations. We were going to travel to the place where we had longed to spend our honeymoon but couldn't afford to at the time. Unable to face those closest to me for whom the date held meaning, I chose to go on a holiday over that period to somewhere we would never have gone together. It was far removed from any civilisation and I did manage to 'lose' the date – but I also wept many bitter tears for what 'should have been'.

I remember dates, but I tend now not to be quite so hung up on them because over the years I've learned that I live in the 'here and now'. There are alternative ways of celebrating and remembering that may take at least some of the anguish away and turn a negative approach to dates into a positive one. Plan ways to commemorate significant dates in advance. For an anniversary or birthday you might:

- 'Buy' your loved one a gift in the form of a donation to charity. This may mean that you can commemorate the date in a way that might have given them pleasure and you may be able to affix their name to it in a way that will give pleasure to others, depending on how much you have to spend. You might plant a few rose bushes or a tree in their favourite park with their name attached; or even endow a park bench.
- Give a donation of a book or books by his or her favourite author, or on a favourite subject, to a hospital library or hospice with a name certificate inside – something along the lines of – In loving memory of . . . on her/his birthday.
- Plan an intimate evening of 'life-celebration' with a group of close family or friends who knew your beloved one well. Tell them this is not to be a miserable wake, but a party to commemorate their

life and ask them to bring along any pictures or other memorabilia they may have of the happy times you all shared.

It may help to commemorate the anniversary of a death as well as to give thanks for life. Jewish people remember the anniversary of death with yahrzeit – translated, the word means 'time of year'. On that date, we light candles which burn for twenty-five hours – the light of life continues in the midst of grief. Those of other faiths could go to church and light a candle there in memory and give thanks for a life well-loved. For those who do not believe, give yourself time to sit quietly and talk to the one who has died from the depths of your heart.

How you can help yourself

Everybody's circumstances are different. Some people need to have their own time and space in which to come to terms with the difference in their lives. Others need to be surrounded by people they know and trust. Some people run from one friend to another, from one activity to another, never stopping for fear of needing to confront the situation. However, the longer you leave it, the harder it will be. You do need to confront your loss in order to be able to go forward.

- Ask yourself whether or not you need or want help beyond your own immediate circle. Sometimes, you may find it far easier to talk to a total stranger than a friend or relative. Contact your vicar, priest, religious leader or CRUSE, the bereavement counselling service who will be able to put you in touch with someone in your area who is qualified to help. Beware of un-trained 'counsellors'. They can do more harm than good.
- You may need to 'complete' the end for yourself. You may have been lucky enough to say all the things you wanted to say. If not – and this is the case for most of us – it may help to write a diary or a letter to the person who has died, saying all those things you want to say, just as though you are talking to them.

This is for your eyes (and their souls) only, so you can say exactly what you want. If you are angry, say you are angry. If you feel cheated or deceived, tell your loved one so. Be really honest on paper about your relationship. Leave the rose-tinted glasses somewhere else. This is you talking to you, about you, to help yourself.

- Don't be bullied. It is very easy to accept 'good advice' and to act on it when you are feeling vulnerable but to regret it later. Only do the things you really want to do.
- *Do not make any major, life-changing plans, for example, to move or to give up work, if you don't want to, for at least two years.*

Finding others in the same boat

When you find the time to draw breath following the initial shock of bereavement – and death always comes as a shock whether you expect it or not – you may feel that you are literally the *only* person in the whole world facing the problems you are now experiencing.

Whether you have lost one parent and are an only child left to deal with an elderly, grieving and possibly truculent survivor, whether you have lost a partner of just a few years and are fighting to cope for yourself and young children, whether you have lost a brother, sister or a lifelong close friend, are facing living alone for the first time in your life, or are bereaved as a result of a murder, a suicide or AIDS, death is a terribly lonely experience. But I promise you that you are not the only one, and the best person to offer you some kind of consolation is somebody else in the same boat. Your doctor may well know of an organisation that can help you meet others in a similar situation. For example, the Lesbian and Gay Bereavement Project, which runs from Colindale Hospital, Colindale Avenue, in North London, provides advice and support for homosexual people on the death of a partner. You can contact them on 020 7403 5969 or visit their website: www.rememberance. org.uk.

Survivors of Bereavement by Suicide runs from Centre 88,

Saner Street, Anlaby Road, Hull HU3 2TR. Their national helpline is 0870 241 3337, which will refer you to your local group.

Support after Murder and Manslaughter list their *raison d'être* as offering understanding and support to families and friends who have been bereaved as a result of murder and manslaughter, through the mutual support of others who have suffered a similar tragedy. You can call their helpline on 020 7735 3838 or visit their website: www.sam.org.uk.

There are many other such organisations, offering support to those whose loved ones have died from specific diseases such as epilepsy or genetic disorders such as Down's Syndrome. It is only when you are among people who know exactly what you are talking about that you can find some kind of release.

4

Religion

'To every thing there is a season, and a time to every purpose under the heaven: a time to be born, and a time to die.'

Ecclesiastes 3:1–8

When death occurs within a family or a community, people who may not have sought or practised organised religion in years may find comfort and solace in the traditions of worship, embraced by the arms of their God and their community. Of course, there are those who are 'turned off' religion when someone they love dies. They wonder how there can be a God when that God is so unfair to them, so insensitive to their needs.

At times of personal or national disaster, outpourings of grief and communal worship bring many people both together and to their God. Turning for help, strength and forbearance to endure their suffering to an omnipresent Being shifts the burden of responsibility from their shoulders. When Diana, Princess of Wales was so tragically killed in that terrible car accident in Paris, candles were lit and prayers were said for her soul, and for the future of her sons and her family, in places of worship around the world. People of all faiths, colours and creeds mourned her death as though she were a member of their own family. Strangers cried on one another's shoulders. They travelled from all over Great Britain to attend her funeral, carrying flowers to lay at Kensington Palace in her memory.

How do I know this? Because I was on a train in the early hours on the day of her funeral, covering the way in which people were coping and the way in which they were mourning, on behalf of a Sunday newspaper. People sat silently throughout arduous journeys, speaking in whispers, queuing for refreshments for total strangers, drawn together by their mutual grief. People of different faiths sat on those trains praying silently together, each according to their own belief and offered small acts of kindness in the name of faith and in Princess Diana's memory.

Such community spirit and belief in the power of prayer to help a departing soul on its way was again evident at the time of the terrorist attack on the heart of the USA, proving once more that death knows no religious or national boundaries. No one can fail to have been moved by the outpourings of sorrow and grief at the interdenominational prayer services held in places of worship worldwide in memory of those who perished in the cataclysmic New York Twin Towers disaster on 11 September 2001. One of Britain's leading Islamic clerics, Sheikh Dr Zaki Badawi of London's Muslim college, for example, joined with members of the West London Reform Synagogue for a Friday-night, Sabbath service. Unlikely worship partners, perhaps, but true brothers in grief.

Furthermore, leading Christian, Hindu, Sikh, Jewish, Muslim and Buddhist clergymen took part in a service of community affirmation organised by the City of Westminster, alongside the Queen, the Prime Minister, the American Ambassador and other dignitaries at the memorial service held at St Paul's Cathedral just three days after the event. Pews in churches, temples, synagogues and mosques were filled to overflowing by people at prayer. The millions of individual candles lit in memory of those whose lives were snuffed out by this tragedy were symbols of the flame of everlasting life, of hope and of remembrance. Those carpets of flowers laid in Union Square in Manhattan, so reminiscent of those laid at Kensington Palace at the time of Princess Diana's death, were further symbols of hope that God, Christ, Ishwara or Allah or whatever other name you call the Almighty will let their souls rest in peace.

Comfort through belief

'At a time when everyone is feeling a deep sense of loss, religion offers a source of comfort through belief,' says Caroline, whose sister died from a brain tumour in her twenties. 'I found the clergy we dealt with were well-trained in ways to care for us, the bereaved. They said and did all the right things. This was the second time I have experienced the death of a very close relative. My father died several years ago. But thanks to my vicar's kindness and expertise in such a situation, I discovered not only a sense of comfort but a feeling of hope in the midst of grief and belief in the afterlife. The most poignant thing was that I learned to respect and understand that just as God gives life, so, I now believe, He has the right to take it. Learning this took away some of the personal responsibility I felt when my sister was dying. I felt so guilty because there was nothing I could do to prevent the inevitability of her death. I gradually came to feel that although my mother gave birth to my sister, her life was ultimately the gift of God and she was merely on loan to us. When I explained this to my mother, she confessed that she, too, had been blaming herself for my sister's death. She had been asking herself: "Did I do something wrong? What could I have done to prevent her being so ill? Should I have noticed something was wrong sooner?" Listening to what our vicar said, both privately and during her funeral service, removed that feeling of guilt. Both my mum and I accepted then that God wanted my sister's soul and that was the reason she died.'

Not everyone feels this way, though. Susan says that her father lost his faith when her mother died. Once a practising Christian, she now admits that she rarely attends church, and explains: 'My father wanted to know how the God he had believed in and worshipped unquestioningly all his life could possibly have let my mother suffer the pain of the illness that finally killed her. He couldn't find an answer to "Why?", so when he died, my sister and I decided on a Humanist funeral for him. We felt that is what he would have wanted and took comfort from fulfilling what we felt were his wishes and his beliefs. There was no priest. The eulogies were given by people who had known him well during his life. They spoke about his personality, about the people he had loved and the reasons he had loved them. As the coffin was brought into the crematorium hall, we played the Goons' "Ying Tong Song", his favourite music, and everyone fell about laughing. That's what we felt he would have wanted.'

The bare fact of the matter is that whatever you do or do not believe, I personally think that funerals and grieving are for the living as well as helping the souls of the dead on their final journey. The words of prayer, whether spoken out loud or silently, offer a sense of being able to 'do' something for the deceased. The Jewish tradition of saying prayers in synagogue morning and evening for eleven months following the death of a parent, sibling or child enables their closest blood relatives to continue to be active on their behalf and in their memory. It also accords a way of remembering and celebrating a life, according to the guidelines by which the dead person once lived.

Similarly, the act of lighting candles on birthdays, special anniversaries, and on the anniversary of a loved one's death – common in so many world religions – is a way of remaining pro-active. In his book *The Laws of Life*, a guide to traditional Jewish practice at times of bereavement, Rabbi Jonathan Wittenberg quotes the Book of Proverbs, reminding mourners of how the flame of a candle is likened to the spirit: 'A lamp of the Lord is the human soul' (20:27). 'The flame is often understood to represent that part of a person which cannot be extinguished. The light indicates how people can illumine the lives of those whom they have loved, long after they have died in body,' he says.

Funeral services

Whatever your religious beliefs, the very act of having a funeral service, whether of a religious or humanist nature, offers a means of finishing business – in this case the 'business' of a life. This is what makes it so much harder for those who (like the survivors and the mourners of those killed in catastrophes such as Aberfan, Lockerbie and the recent US terrorist attacks, where there are no bodies to bury or graves to visit) may find it almost impossible to come to terms with, or even believe in, the death of their loved ones without some kind of ceremony. Where there can be no funeral, it is often important to create some kind of ritual to offer people a channel through which to express their grief.

Often, people who have not practised organised religion for many years during their lifetime may find a need to return to the faith of their earlier life when death nears. Sometimes it is a decision to give their loved one a religious burial, based not necessarily on their wishes but on the beliefs of family who want to 'do the right thing' in their memory. Some people are slightly superstitious, believing they should bury somebody according to the faith into which they were born 'just in case'. They are taking out an 'insurance policy' against the possibility that they are wrong in their lack of belief – if this gives them comfort, then why not? Mourning, whether formal mourning according to a religious practice or informal mourning according to the needs of an individual, is an outlet for the grief of the survivors. If what is done in memory of the dead person brings comfort to the living, it can only be a positive outcome at a very sad time. Unless someone has left spoken or written instructions for their own funeral, possibly in their will, their funeral will be about what the family believe they should do rather than what the dead person might have chosen for themselves.

The Reverend Nigel Hartley, vicar of five small parishes in Suffolk, England, including Great Finborough, Harlston, Buxhall, Onehouse and Shelland, explains: 'When someone is dying, the mourning of those around them can start before they die. The family know they are losing someone and that is the moment they first need support, although often they don't ask for it soon enough. Ideally, religious leaders should be involved before someone dies, if it is known that that is what is happening, but it rarely happens because of people's reticence and embarrassment dealing with the whole subject of death.'

Revd Hartley says that when he is faced with helping a family deal with death, and at a time when he is arranging a funeral, he will generally try to speak to at least two relatives of the person who has died in order to build an overall picture of them as they were seen and known by their loved ones. 'Funerals and memorial services need to have a very personal touch,' he says. 'The mourners need to know that someone is taking a deep interest in the person who has died and I generally start by trying to find out about the beginning of their life, asking about their parents, where they went to school, about their growing-up years, their marriages, and where children come into the picture. I am aiming to get the family to say something in their own words about the deceased. I generally try to spend at least two hours with the bereaved family before conducting a Christian burial.'

This is the time when mourners may derive great solace from hearing the fine attributes of a loved one eulogised in public. Unlike the story that is told of the funeral of a very unpopular, difficult old man who had no close family to mourn him. Feeling sad at his lonely state in death, a distant relative managed to muster a few people to his funeral. The vicar, who knew neither the dead man nor any member of his family, led a prayer. He stood on the lectern and the congregation held their collective breath, waiting for something to be said about the crotchety old boy. 'Before I continue with the service,' said the vicar, 'would anyone like to say a few words about the deceased?' Silence. The embarrassed vicar repeated the question. Still silence. Finally, the frustrated parson insisted: 'I'm unable to carry on with this service unless someone says something.' A tiny voice piped up from the back of the church: 'His brother was worse.'

Discovering who, what and how the dead person lived, so that the knowledge can be shared at a funeral, is common to most faiths.

It is interesting to discover, therefore, that many Christian vicars, priests and lay leaders envy the guidelines for mourning rituals laid down by the Jewish, Hindu and Muslim faiths which suggest periods of deep mourning are followed by periods of lesser mourning in which other celebrations are kept to a minimum. 'It is a shame that such set periods to allow mourning to take place openly are not laid down within Christianity,' regrets Revd Hartley. 'In my experience, it is a great help to the mourners not to have to excuse themselves when they feel unable to participate in partying following the death of a loved one.'

John Brentnall, a teacher of Comparative Religion at the University of Suffolk Interfaith Resource in Ipswich says: 'There is an ambiguity about the object of religious funerals. They do three things.

1. They are a thanksgiving for life.
2. They optimise the notion that the dead person is now with God.
3. They afford an opportunity for those who are left to affect God's judgement about the fate of the soul of the deceased, through their fervent prayers on behalf of the departed soul. They fear that otherwise the afterlife may all go horribly wrong for the dead person.

'Funerals, particularly religious funerals, are a warning to everyone to remember their own mortality.

'The world's main religions share many points in common, including the words of some prayers, but in many ways they also manifest vast differences in religious beliefs and practices.

'There was a time when cremation was quite unacceptable in the Catholic Church, although it is now becoming far more acceptable. Orthodox Christians do not believe in cremation because they believe that the body is a temple of the Holy Spirit in life and as such will be inhabited by the Holy Spirit again at the time of the resurrection. Orthodox Jews do not believe in cremation either. They believe that the body must be "returned to the earth as it was" and buried intact. Muslims' attitude to grieving concentrates on the resurrection,' he says. Cremation, however, is central to the belief of Hindus, who believe the concept of 'ashes to ashes', as the Bible puts it, or 'from nothing to nothing' as the Hindu religious leader, Deva Samaroo, says.

Different faiths – what is expected of me?

The emotions engendered by death may be the same, but the rituals, however, differ in different religions. It may be helpful to know what to do or what to expect when friends, colleagues or even family members of a different faith or culture lose a loved one. Christian, Humanist, Jew, Sikh, Hindu, Muslim or Buddhist, each has their own ritual burial and mourning procedures.

It is important to know whether or not you are expected to attend a funeral. Should you send flowers, make a donation to charity, or do nothing in memory of the deceased?

It is clearly impossible to cover all the rituals followed by all religions in a book such as this one and this is only a very general guide. Above and beyond religious differences, all that really matters is offering consolation to mourners. People who are suffering following a bereavement will appreciate that you are trying to understand what they are doing and why – and that in itself is a comfort. Mourners rarely remember *every* person who came to the funeral or attended other religious ceremonies or who wrote or phoned their condolences. But they will *often* remember those who didn't come, didn't write and didn't make any contact. *If you want to help and don't know how, don't be afraid to ask.*

Food

Whatever their religion, it is generally customary for friends and family to join the mourners for some kind of refreshment following a funeral, which may be a catered wake organised by the funeral directors or family. Family and friends may repair to the home of a member of the family following the funeral service. If this is the case, ask one of the chief mourners whether help is needed to prepare a meal or snack. If you are not of the same faith as those who mourn and feel awkward about attending a religious service of another faith, such an offer may be more helpful than attendance at the funeral service itself.

Religious practices in different faiths

This is a complex subject – and if you need to know more than the brief outline I am able to offer here, don't be embarrassed to ask your friends, even in their time of grief, if you don't understand the ritual. They are sure to appreciate your concern.

Buddhists

Buddhist funeral services and mourning traditions may vary in both length and content, according to the origins of the Buddhist practice. Funerals of Japanese Buddhists, for example, generally resemble a Christian funeral with a eulogy and prayers at a funeral home. The service will last about an hour and a quarter. If the Sri Lankan, Cambodian or Thai traditions are being followed, however, there may be up to three ceremonies, each lasting about forty-five minutes. The first, held within two days of the death, will be held at the home of the bereaved. At the second, generally held between two and five days following the death, monks will conduct a ceremony at the funeral home, and the third, held seven days after the burial or cremation, will see monks leading a ceremony, either at the home of the bereaved or at a temple. This last ceremony, known as a 'merit transference', seeks to generate good energy for the deceased in his or her new incarnation.

Visitors generally attend the first ceremony. The casket will be open and relatives and friends of the deceased pay homage to the body. Buddhism deems viewing the body to be a valuable reminder of the impermanence of life, and those who come to pay their respects are expected to bow to it as a sign of appreciation of the lesson that life does not last for ever. All Buddhist sects quote from the Sutras, the collected sayings of Buddha.

Christians

Practising Christians follow no particular time scale for burial or mourning. Funerals are organised to allow time for loved ones to travel from far and near to pay their last respects to the deceased and their relatives. Burial or cremation may be arranged by either funeral directors or individuals but generally occurs within a week to ten days, to give people time to make the necessary arrangements, particularly when there are family and friends living long distances away.

But, as the Church of England has become less formal, so funeral procedures have become less standardised. Though the grand 'set piece' of an old-fashioned East End of London funeral, such as the one conducted for the infamous Kray twins, complete with magnificent hearses drawn by horses resplendent in white plumage and followed by feast-style wakes, is becoming less common (certainly in large English cities), such a funeral has the advantage of permitting the most stoical individuals to express their grief openly and without embarrassment. Certainly many British people find grief embarrassing and prefer to acknowledge death only in the immediacy of the crisis. Once the funeral is over, they find it easier to 'deal' with those who have been bereaved by hoping that they have 'got over it' and expecting life to carry on as before with no time permitted for open sorrow. Here, ethnic origins play a large part.

The old stiff upper-lip British tradition still rules in England. Visible grieving is acceptable until the burial, after which those in mourning are expected to do their crying in private and show a public face of 'business as usual'. Thankfully, bereavement counselling is becoming far more widely available and acceptable now throughout the UK as well as in the US, permitting those whose loved ones have died to grieve publicly for more than a week or two (see the next chapter).

Private funerals are also becoming increasingly common in both Great Britain and the US. Only those invited attend the ceremony and often there is a simple church service followed by interment. The funeral directors can generally advise both those who attend and those who don't whether or not flowers are acceptable, and, afterwards, these floral tributes may be left on the grave or taken to a hospital or hospice. Often, the funeral directors will know if the bereaved or close relations have indicated that they would prefer charitable donations to flowers – and may suggest a suitable charity. After some light refreshments, it will be 'back to normal' for the mourners. Often, and especially where there has been a private funeral, a public memorial service may be held later to commemorate the life of the deceased, with personal eulogies and acts of faith.

Exceptions to the British way of mourning occur within the Irish communities. In both north and southern Ireland, among Protestants as well as Catholics, there is a prevailing belief in giving the dead a 'decent' send-off, with high regard paid to the rituals surrounding the death, and with great respect paid to the removal of the body by the undertaker. Mass attendance at a funeral is seen as a communal duty. Everyone goes to offer their support for the bereaved. Afterwards, at the wake there will be much eating, and even more drinking and eulogising of the deceased. It is a way of celebrating life, and of allowing those who have lost a relative or friend to share in the general feeling of sorrow and sadness. At Afro-Caribbean funerals, there is generally a great deal of spiritual music and grieving is much more open and communally shared.

Until December 2000, in the UK, there were no formal prayers or ritual support systems for visiting the bereaved following the funeral as there are in many other world religions, although Revd Hartley and other caring priests and vicars generally followed up on the welfare of bereaved families. The Church of England has since introduced a new prayer book, *Common Worship: Pastoral Services*, the funeral provisions of which provide services and prayers from before the death to well into the mourning period (including the memorial service).

The old tradition of prayers on the third, sixth and ninth days after the death have disappeared. (In her book *Dying Well*, written to guide health-care professionals through the different rituals surrounding dying, Rabbi Julia Neuberger attributes this to the old, anti-Catholic feeling.)

Once the burial and ceremonial rites are over, those who have been bereaved are often left very much to their own devices. Vi Neale-Smith's experience is just one example of how isolated and bereft people in such a situation may feel: 'As a regular churchgoer, I expected help and support from my fellow worshippers at church,' say Mrs Neale-Smith, whose husband died sixteen years ago. 'I didn't get it. I went to church once or twice after his death, but the people I had worked alongside in various church groups for years didn't acknowledge me when I needed them most. I found that the people who helped me were my friends from the yoga class I ran. It was a long time before I felt able to go back to worship in church on a regular basis.'

Organ donation is encouraged throughout the Christian faith. The Christian Church teaches that: 'There can be no greater love than for a man to lay down his life for his friend,' (John 15:13) and, in modern times, this has come to be understood that the Lord would surely welcome the sharing of organs no longer needed with those where the quality of life can be enhanced and lengthened as a result of organ donation.

Humanists

Most humanists are cremated. The eulogies will probably be read by family and friends before cremation. 'My sister and I felt that we wanted my father's funeral to be more personal than my mother's Christian burial,' says Susan. 'I felt he had a much better send-off. We played music he loved. We read from books he'd enjoyed during his life and the service was personal to him and to the way he had lived.' There are no rules about the kind of music that may be played at a Humanist funeral or who should play it. Each service is as individual as those who arrange it and can be as meaningful as any religious traditional service of whatever faith. The uninitiated should be prepared for the unexpected!

Hindus

Hindus believe that the soul or spirit, known as *atman*, is unborn and undying. They believe that the soul is the eternal flame which simply changes its 'clothing', i.e. the body. At the moment of death, the *atman* passes into a new carnation and the form of this incarnation depends on how the *atman* has performed in his previous life. This reincarnation continues over many lifetimes until it has realised the true nature of reality and finally becomes a free soul to be with Brahma or Ishwara, the one, all-encompassing, omnipotent, omnipresent God.

The funeral and mourning process are complicated. Hindus, however, would never countenance lack of ceremony for lack of a family's ability to finance a proper funeral. Where a family cannot afford a full, traditional funeral, the community will club together to meet the expenses.

The mortal remains of the deceased will generally be taken back to the place where they once lived. Cremation usually takes place within twenty-four hours. (The tradition for cremation immediately following death stems from the need to dispose of bodies quickly in the hot Indian climate in order to prevent infection.)

Following death, and prior to cremation, certain orthodox puritanical sections of the Hindu faith will perform the first part of what is known as the shraadha ceremony. During this ceremony, holy water from the river Ganges is mixed with ordinary water. The oldest son or male relative will place a few drops of this water on the lips of the deceased as the last 'feed', before the body is dressed and decorated, ready for a public viewing.

The Hindu funeral ceremony is the last of the sixteen rituals or samskaras that are performed by Hindus from the time of conception to the time of death. The final samskara is called the anthesti (antim) samskara. In India, the oldest son or senior male member of the family will light the funeral pyre, but in other parts of the world where such a practice is impractical, this tradition will be followed symbolically by the lighting of a candle. Prayers are offered to Ishwara that the passage of the soul to its new carnation should be peaceful. Following the cremation, there will be another ceremony at home where food will be served. Hindus value physical expressions of warmth such as hand-holding and hugging at such a time.

Hindus wear white for mourning and also at the funeral. When a woman wears white, it denotes that she has been widowed.

Like some other faiths, Hindus believe in community mourning. Mourning may continue for forty days, or for anything from eleven to thirteen months. The length of the mourning period is at the family's discretion. On the tenth and thirteenth day after death, the second and third part of the shraddha ceremony will be performed as some believe that it helps the soul on its journey to merge with Brahma. (Some Hindus, however, may only follow a celebration of remembrance, called havan, a week or so following cremation.) Both these ceremonies will be repeated in the ninth, eleventh and thirteenth month after cremation and will mark the final acts of mourning.

Jews

The Jewish funeral and mourning period are times of public grieving, too. Everything that is done is done both to honour the memory of the dead and to comfort those who mourn their death. Orthodox Jews do not believe in cremation although many Reform and Liberal Jews do cremate their dead. The faces of those who have died are always covered immediately after death as a sign of respect. The body is never laid out for public viewing, as this is seen as mocking the dead. It is bathed and clothed in a white shroud and placed in a simple, unadorned box for burial.

Where possible, burial will generally take place within twenty-four hours of death. As with other religions originating in hot climates, this was a matter of hygiene which has become traditional. The body is attended at all times before burial by a 'watcher' who guards it and who may neither eat nor drink in its presence. At the cemetery, the ritual of 'keriah', tearing the garment, is performed, traditionally by a close friend or sometimes the sexton. The clothing of a spouse, parent, child or sibling of the deceased is torn, with the tear being made on the left-hand side over the heart for parents and on the right-hand side for other relatives. As the mourner completes the tear themself, they will recite a prayer accepting God's decree. When the mourners return from the cemetery following the burial, friends will have prepared a symbolic meal of condolence, consisting of a hard-boiled egg, as the symbol of new life, a piece of bread, usually a bagel, which has no beginning and no end, as the symbol of everlasting life, and a piece of salted herring as the symbol of tears that have been shed.

For the next seven days, a period of intense mourning or shiva, first-degree relatives sit on low chairs wearing soft shoes or slippers. Bathing, putting on fresh clothes, shaving or doing anything else for comfort or pleasure is forbidden. Don't be shocked by their appearance!

Each morning, first-degree mourners will attend prayers at synagogue. In the evening, family, friends and the community will come to the shiva house where a 'quorum' of ten people (men only in orthodox communities) will gather for prayers and to recite the 'kaddish'. This is not, as is generally believed, a prayer for the departed person's soul, but rather a prayer glorying the goodness of God. Mirrors in the house will be covered to avoid vanity. Visitors will come throughout the day to offer comfort, food and care for their daily needs, to the bereaved throughout the shiva period. People who are sitting shiva are not permitted to thank those who come to offer practical help as well as comfort and prayer. It may appear confusing when non-Jews discover that although the tradition is for orthodox Jews to sit shiva for seven days, some Jewish people choose to 'sit' for just one or two.

For the thirty days following the funeral, orthodox mourners will not shave. They will avoid parties, the theatre, concerts, or anywhere music is played. In orthodox communities, a son, brother or father will attend synagogue twice daily to recite the kaddish for twelve months. In non-orthodox communities, this practice may also be followed by daughters, sisters and mothers. But while blood relatives mourn for eleven months, at which time a memorial stone will be consecrated in memory of the dead person and a final memorial service held at the graveside, spouses are directed to mourn for only thirty days. The Jewish religion teaches that men and women should have partners and should not be alone once the initial mourning period is over. Jewish people believe that the soul returns to God who gave it and that the souls of all Jewish people will be resurrected in Jerusalem when the Messiah comes.

Never send flowers to a Jewish funeral. If you wish to do something to mark the life of the departed, you may send donations to a chosen charity.

Muslims

With over thirty million Muslims in Europe, excluding Turkey, Islam is one of the fastest-growing religions in the world. The cycle of mourning lasts a year.

Only Muslims may prepare fellow Muslims for burial in a shroud, sometimes one which the deceased themselves may have brought back from Mecca. Muslims are always buried, never cremated. Their burial will be carried out within twenty-four hours if possible, again a tradition emanating from the climate in the countries of origin. The immediate family generally stay at home for three days following the funeral and the grave is visited on Fridays for the first forty days. Alms are given to the poor in honour of the person who has died. Muslim widows are expected to stay at home for 130 days following the death of a partner, dressed in simple clothes and wearing no jewellery.

For the first month, the family observes deep mourning and, during this time, visitors are warmly welcomed to support those who have been bereaved, to bring gifts of food, and to speak of the meritorious deeds of the departed. Once the initial forty days of mourning are over, those who follow Islam faith rarely visit graves.

Sikhs

A peace-loving people who believes in one God, the Ten Gurus, the Adi Granth (holy book) and other scriptures and teachings of the Ten Gurus, Sikhs believe in the cycle of reincarnation and that certain actions and attachments bind the soul to this cycle. They believe that by being aware of death throughout life, and by being deeply prayerful, they may become detached and righteous enough to break the cycle of birth and death and return to God.

Because, like Hindus, they believe the soul never dies, Sikhs do not mourn the death of a loved one, and all the ceremonies commemorating a death include much prayer to help the soul to be released from the bonds of reincarnation and become at one with God again.

For those who practise the Sikh faith, death is not an end but the beginning of the next life and again, like Hindus, they believe that the next life is based upon the quality and deeds of the life of the person who has just died.

In Rehat Maryada, a guide to the Sikh way of life, the practices to be followed in death include the firm insistence that no rituals derived from other religions, or from any other source, should be performed when a death occurs. Sikhs are ordered to find comfort in the reading of the Adi Granth and meditating.

Professor Harbindar Singh, President of the World Congress of Religions, explains that when a death occurs, it is a duty to cremate the body as quickly as possible. 'Of course, in Britain, this may entail waiting a day or two,' he says. 'Before the cremation takes place, we take the body to the Sikh temple Goddurgawara and there the priests pray for the departed soul to find a place in heaven. From there, the body is taken on to the crematorium where a priest or lay priest prays for the departed soul. There is a special prayer, which is said standing and which call on the names of all the Gurus to invoke God's blessing. Then a special hymn is sung before the cremation.'

Sikhs do not express grief at the death of their loved ones because they believe that the soul continues to live in a new incarnation. 'Excessive grief is forbidden because it is written in the holy book: "If you cry, cry in love for the soul of the departed and not because you are suffering",' he says.

As in other faiths, there will be a eulogy following cremation, which is followed by prayers. When somebody dies, it is customary for friends and neighbours to bring food so that the mourners can concentrate on prayers and not worry about cooking.

Visitors are welcome to offer their condolences following the cremation service and a continuous reading of the Siri Guru Granth Sahib is read in the Gurmukhi language for forty-eight hours. If the book is read in English, the period of reading can be extended to seventy-two hours. People take turns in reading the text. If breaks are taken, the prayer reading can last for four or five days. There are other ceremonies to console the family. 'In happy times, Sikh families invite the outside world to join them in celebration. In times of trouble and death, it is incumbent on the relatives and friends to be present and share their pain,' says Professor Harbindar Singh. 'All religions have much in common. In St John's Gospel, it says that believers should worship not the paper but the words spoken by the prophets.'

5

Counselling

Do you need counselling? Do you want counselling? Why should you have counselling?

It's amazing how many people advise you to 'go for counselling' when they themselves have no idea what it is, why you should have it, what it entails or what it may or may not do to help you. It can almost sound like an excuse to get you off their backs! Then there are those who question why you might consider 'all this counselling rubbish'. People often say: 'Lots of people died in the war and their relatives didn't get counselled' – as though somehow accepting counselling is a strange self-indulgence at a time when you really shouldn't be pampering yourself.

Soon after my losses, a number of people, including religious leaders and my doctor, suggested I needed 'counselling'. It was just about the last thing I wanted – at the time! Why would I, who had so often written about other people's problems, need to ask someone else about a way to cope with this situation? Like many other people who've been bereaved, I was convinced I could do it myself. I knew the theory, so all I had to do was put it into practice. After bereavement, particularly a 'shock' bereavement, most of us go into auto-pilot. We do what has to be done because we have no choice. We make the necessary appointments. Write the lists. Do what other people suggest and what we think is 'right'. Keep busy, ever-moving. The one thing we rarely do is give ourselves the luxury of time to grieve properly because, with so many practicalities to be dealt with, once the intial shock is over, there is no time.

Six months down the line, when the essentials were done, I found time to 'feel' again. I can only explain this sensation as the sensation you get when you've been resting on your knees so long that your feet go totally numb and then suddenly you are assailed by an agonising attack of pins and needles.

I was so angry, so frustrated and so depressed all at once. I thought I was going mad, literally. I really couldn't understand how I could be so furious with someone who was dead, for committing the act of dying. I couldn't cope with my muddled emotions. One minute, I wanted people around me, the next, I wanted to be alone. I couldn't see any point in carrying on with living. Yet I didn't have the courage to let go and kill myself. I suppose I was verging on suicidal, but I had my daughters to consider.

Then when I was given the magazine with an article by a woman who, like me, had lost a young husband, I started to read it – and was amazed to find I could have been reading about myself. This woman had been as angry, as guilty, as depressed, as frustrated and as confused as I was. I felt enormous relief to discover I wasn't losing my sanity after all.

Philip Hodson, Head of Media at the BAC, the British Association of Counselling, says: 'Accepting counselling following bereavement or any other life crisis is hard work for both sides. It is demanding, it is tough, it is difficult and it pulls no punches. It tells you that unhappiness is unavoidable and that crying never hurt anybody – indeed, crying is one of the best relaxation remedies you will find.'

A great many books and pamphlets set time limits on grief. They suggest that after the first four weeks, the numbness wears off – and that for the first three months you may be very angry. I think time limits are rubbish. What I feel like six months down the line may be similar (but never *exactly* the same) as someone else will describe two years onwards. What I say or do now, or years away from the situation, may be the way someone else reacts after six weeks.

'Time is only a healer if you use it to help yourself grieve. Otherwise, time just passes and you bury yourself in those feelings of grief and will emerge fresh as a daisy seventy years on,' Philip Hodson quips. 'However, there is one time limit I will admit to: after about two years, most people do feel more adjusted. The period of two years is significant because by that time, you will have lived through two whole cycles of seasons and that means that everything the dead person represented to you in terms of things they did and their relationship to you will have been remembered at least once around. You know you've lost the person who used to cut the grass and you've learned how to do it yourself. You've learned how to replace the home-made Christmas cake. You have also lost the disagreeable parts of the person who has died, so that, even despite the death, you may feel quite pleased and relieved – and then perhaps feel guilty. But by the end of the second year, you need no longer think back to this time last year – or last time we did that together.'

No one, not even a counsellor trained to the highest standards, can give you set time limits on grief, in the way they can tell you that a cold will last seven days. You can't say that the numbness will last this long; the anger this long. Acceptance will come after a year. It will only come when that stage of grieving is right for you. As Dame Cicely Saunders, founder of the modern hospice movement, once said: 'There is no timetable for the human heart.'

The important thing about counsellors is that good ones won't tell you what to do, or, for that matter, how to do it. They don't attempt to 'bend' your thoughts or emotions. Good bereavement counsellors should lead you through the mire of death and its sludgy aftermath to a safe and dry path where you can figure things out for yourself.

Where can I find a trained counsellor?

There are many bereavement charities in the UK. CRUSE is the largest, with 180 local branches throughout the UK. It offers help to people bereaved by death, regardless of their age, nationality or belief. Not only does CRUSE offer a free counselling service for bereaved people, but also opportunities for contact with others through bereavement support groups and advice or information on practical matters.

This is personal, confidential help, backed by a wide range of publications. There is also a monthly newsletter for bereaved people which is available for a nominal subscription. In addition, CRUSE arranges training courses for those who work either in a professional or lay capacity with the bereaved. They are totally professional and if you entrust them to help you or anyone you love, you can be sure that the care and attention you receive will be utterly capable, skilled and efficient. CRUSE counsellors receive ongoing training.

There are other, equally professional bodies with trained counsellors available to help specific needs. The British Association for Counselling has a list of more than twenty thousand institutional members. You can find them on the BAC website www.counselling.co.uk or through their headquarters at 1 Regent Place, Rugby, Warwickshire CV21 2PJ (telephone 0870 443 5252).

Those who have been bereaved as a result of murder or manslaughter, those who have lost loved ones through suicide, or in the Holocaust, all have very specialised needs – as do those who have lost children. Specialised counselling is available from organisations such as Support After Murder and Manslaughter (Cranmer House, 39 Brixton Road, London SW9 6DZ; telephone helpline: 020 7735 3838) and Survivors of Bereavement by Suicide (Centre 88, Saner Street, Anlaby Road, Hull HU3 2TR). The Compassionate Friends (53 North Street, Bristol BS1 3EN; telephone helpline: 0117 953 9639, manned seven days a week from 10 a.m. to 4 p.m. and 6.30 p.m. to 10.30 p.m.) offers support and friendship for bereaved parents and their families from those who have been similarly bereaved, and the Child Death Helpline (open 365 days a year – Monday, Wednesday and Friday from 10 a.m. to 1 p.m. and every evening from 7 p.m. to 10 p.m.) which runs from an office at the Great Ormond Street Hospital for Sick Children to help and guide those whose sick children have died. Their free telephone helpline number is 0800 282 986. The Foundation for the Study of

Infant Death offers support to parents who have experienced the sudden, unexpected death of infants as a result of Cot Death Syndrome and is based at Artillery House, 11–19 Artillery Row, London SW1P 1RT. They run a 24-hour helpline: 020 7233 2090, and a website: www.sids.org.uk/fsid. There are organisations attached to religious bodies such as the Jewish Bereavement Counselling Service, which can offer advice from an in-depth understanding of the customs surrounding death within a religious context, and many local authorities run counselling services.

Whether you choose to accept counselling that is available without charge – or you decide to pay for a private counsellor to help you through your grief, it is vital to check that their qualifications are sound – and that they have undergone structured training under the guidance of expert teachers. If you choose to travel the private route, do try to choose a counsellor who has been recommended rather than finding them through *Yellow Pages*. Anyone can set themselves up as a counsellor by adding a few initials to their name – and currently there is nothing illegal about shutting a shoe shop on Friday and advertising yourself as a therapist on Monday morning. I know of several people who have been 'counselled' by improperly trained counsellors. The experience caused them more harm than good. It is also possible that you may not instantly 'click' with a counsellor and the result can cause you even more pain. If, after a couple of sessions, you are feeling unhappy about the person you are seeing, don't persevere. Cut it there and then. Leave yourself a few weeks to settle down and then, if you feel like it, try again.

Anna says that friends persuaded her to go for counselling after the death of her husband of forty years. It was the final straw. Her mother had died four years previously and her younger brother just two years beforehand. She was deeply depressed, severely distressed and clearly in need of good professional help. It was her sister-in-law who suggested that counselling had helped her and might help Anna too.

'I contacted CRUSE but they had a short waiting list at that time,' Anna explains. 'Having made up my mind to do it, I wanted to get started. I felt if I didn't, I wouldn't go through with it. My doctor recommended a bereavement counsellor who was full of her own misery,' she says. 'I was feeling in the depths of despair and almost the first thing she said was: "It only gets worse." Instead of letting me talk, helping me to accept what had happened, she regaled me with her own experiences, none of which were in the least positive. Every session ended with us both crying – to the point where I felt far worse when she'd gone than when she'd arrived and it used to take me the whole week following her visit to get back to where I had been. It was horrible. It was only when I finally asked her not to come any more that I discovered she had taken a fourteen-week training course, no exams, and that I was one of her first clients. She wasn't fully trained and I don't think she was under any kind of supervision.

'My sister-in-law was mortified. She had been counselled by CRUSE and it had never dawned on her that I would find anyone else. After my experience, I couldn't go through it again. In a way, I wish I could face up to it. I am a very private person by nature. I know that I'm stuck in a depressive rut, but I couldn't go through it all again.'

Your GP or the minister of your parish church, synagogue or mosque will often be able to offer advice on finding a counsellor who will be able to help with your specific needs. (Remember, however, to check out their experience and qualifications.) Private counselling can cost anything between £25 and £50 a session. Philip Hodson believes it's cheap at the price. 'I think it is the best-value product on the market,' he says. 'After all, if you realise that a tarot card reading can cost £75; a good solicitor will charge £200–£250 an hour, and even a London locksmith can charge around £95 to get you through your own front door, £25 seems a small price to pay to help you find a little *peace* of mind.'

Do I, don't I?

In years gone by, no one knew about counselling. Family, friends and neighbours surrounded the bereaved, cushioning them from the brickbats and allowing them to talk their way through and out of their loss. Today, families are spread around the world and despite all the wonders of modern communications, it's not so easy. You can't e-mail your deepest thoughts to someone hundreds or thousands of miles away and feel arms closing round you.

I don't think anyone has the right to tell you, you 'should' have counselling any more than they should tell you that you 'ought' to do anything else. Unlike friends, counsellors are non-judgemental. Well-trained professionals will not and do not tell you what to do. They merely guide you towards discovering ways of making the decisions you need to make for yourself. You can be absolutely sure that counsellors will never gossip about you. Nor will they become your friends in any capacity other than a professional one. People, even those you may have considered closest to you, sometimes have no idea what to say to you as you struggle to cope with your bereavement and all the changes it brings to your life, so they may say nothing at all. A counsellor will listen, lead and help you reach conclusions. Whatever those conclusions, you can be sure that the ultimate choice will be yours.

However, counselling isn't right for everyone: don't get talked into it if it is an avenue you really don't want to explore.

What a trained counsellor will do for you:
- Help you to put your relationship with the person who has died into perspective.
- Help you to accept that he or she is dead.
- Help you to redefine the relationships you have with those around you, in the wake of your loss which may also be the loss of others, i.e. parents, partners, brothers, sisters and children.
- Help you to discover for yourself the things you want – and the things you don't (both emotionally and materialistically) – as opposed to what the person who has died would or would not have wanted for you.
- Help you to discover the person hidden beneath the influence of the dead person.
- Help you to move forward to find new beginnings.

What a trained counseller will NOT do for you:

- No good counsellor will stand in judgement on you – either for your actions, your deeds or thoughts that you may reveal in confidence.
- No counsellor will tell you what to do and what NOT to do.
- No counsellor will tell you what they think of your actions.
- No counsellor will break your confidence.

Circumstances

Most of us lose loved ones as a result of illness or accident. Sometimes, though, grieving and mourning may be more complex – particularly if death has occurred as a result of suicide or murder. There are specialist trained agencies who can help people in such situations, and the help of these highly skilled and motivated counsellors may be particularly useful. There is also a London clinic which specialises in helping children who have been bereaved as a result of murder.

If you are counselled by someone who you don't 'click' with, yet you still feel you need help, say so

Not everyone can get on with, or find empathy with, everyone else. You can clash with a counsellor's personality just as you might clash with the milkman's. This doesn't make for a bad counsellor (or milkman) but perhaps calls for a change of direction. Don't be scared to ring the organising body and explain.

There are people who won't benefit from counselling. This is their choice and they are entitled to make it. If you have a friend who has been bereaved, you can mention that counselling is available and an option, but don't push the point. Immediately after Anton's death, Miriam's doctor suggested that both she and her daughter might benefit from bereavement counselling. Miriam chose not to. It was something she had to work through herself. And she did.

Children

Often children who have lost a parent blame themselves. There are specialist child-trained counsellors who can help and enable them to discover for themselves that they were not responsible. The very young may feel that they've done something 'naughty' so Mummy or Daddy has gone away to punish them. Very often, counselling will help them understand that the death of a parent had nothing to do with any of their actions and that they are entirely blameless.

People tend to believe that children are 'resilient' and that they will cope. Many bottle up their feelings of guilt, taking them into adulthood, and their deep, hidden emotions may blight the rest of their lives. Don't believe that bereaved children will 'manage' or that they have been unaffected by death just because they don't discuss it with you, their surviving parent or grandparent. Professional help, given by specialists trained in a particular field, may be vital to their future health, even if you decline such help yourself.

If you decide to go for it

- Be prepared for some pain but look on it as a birthing. It will hurt, but it will help you towards building the beginning of a new life.
- Be prepared to release all that pent-up anger – it may well be two steps forward and one step back, particularly at the beginning.
- Do it because YOU want to, not because someone else insists it will be 'good' for you.

Befrienders

Another option which may be available, depending on the kind of bereavement you have suffered, is 'befriending'. Befrienders are not trained counsellors. They have generally experienced a similar bereavement to the one you have suffered. I say 'similar' guardedly because although relationships and circumstances may be alike, no two deaths and no two people's reactions to them are ever exactly the same.

The 'befriending' idea was initiated by the Foundation for the Study of Infant Death who have since gone on to instigate other such schemes based on their models with organisations such as Epilepsy Bereaved. Befrienders are generally sensitive people who give of their time voluntarily, and are willing to listen and share their own experience if appropriate. Although they will have attended basic 'preparation days', they are not counsellors and are not able to give medical or legal advice, or indeed intervene on behalf of the people they help. Their basic training is more guideline than formal. They are not trying to replace a bereaved person's family support network, nor will they take the place of old friends by becoming a 'friend'. They offer support, and will themselves be in receipt of support. 'You may never know the value of the support you offer, but don't let this stop you from giving it,' one befriender told the FSID. Many self-help groups do offer befriending support and it is worth making inquiries about it if you feel it may be more helpful to you than formal counselling. But, always remember, the choice is YOURS.

6

When a child dies

The death of someone loved is always sad, no matter what the relationship. But there can be no greater tragedy and no more devastating experience than losing a child.

The day you discover you are expecting a baby is the day you also fall pregnant with possibilities for the future, and with a love for another human being which is like no other. When a baby dies before it is born as a result of miscarriage or still-birth, or dies as a newborn infant, you have lost that relationship almost before it has begun. When the death of a toddler or young child occurs, you lose all your hopes and dreams and plans for that child.

You lose the fulfilment of the guessing games. What would she/ he have looked like as a teenager, when they grew up? Would they have married? Had a family of their own? You lose the chance to be the parent at school, the proud onlooker with a special relationship with that little angel in the school nativity play – and all the other joys, and traumas, which are part of parenthood.

When an adult child dies, you not only lose a unique relationship/ friendship, but a shared wealth of family memories and experience. You also lose the person on whom you might have relied above all others to care for you in later life, as you cared for them in their early months or years.

I cannot tell those who have lost a child that I understand how they feel. I can't. I can only empathise deeply as a result of conversations with parents whose own children have died, who have managed to survive and who now devote much time to bringing comfort to other bereaved mums and dads.

According to the Child Death Helpline twelve thousand children under the age of seventeen die every year in Great Britain. Thousands more die in the eighteen to twenty-four age group. There are no published figures to show how many parents outlive their adult chidlren. Figures are irrelevant. The death of a child is an upset to the natural balance of nature. In the natural scheme of things, parents die before their children. And, the question every bereaved parent asks, is Why? – why my child, why us? Sadly, in most cases, no one will be able to offer you a satisfactory answer to any of these questions. You will almost certainly know the physical reason for your child's death. Genetic illness, acute disease, accident or, for a minority, foul play. Why it was *your* child who was the victim, no one will ever be able to tell you.

The second reaction is 'If only'. If only one had done this, not done that! The truth of the matter is that there is almost certainly *nothing* most parents might have done to prevent the death of their child. Grieving parents may find this hard to believe at the time of their child's death, if ever. As Sheila, a volunteer with Compassionate Friends, a Bristol-based self-help organisation for bereaved parents, with groups countrywide, says: 'Losing a child is against the symmetry of life.'

What's gone wrong

As a parent, when your child dies, you have the right to know exactly what happened as far as the medics can tell you. You may be foxed by terminology, particularly if your child was born dead, or if it was only a tiny baby.

- *Miscarriage* – refers to any baby that dies in the womb up to twenty-four weeks into the pregnancy. Babies who die before the twelfth week are often referred to as *early miscarriages*.

- *Stillbirth* – refers to babies who die before birth but after twenty-four weeks of pregnancy.
- *Neonatal death* – refers to babies who are born alive but who die within the first four weeks of life.
- *Sudden infant death* or *Cot death* – refers to babies up to the age of two years who die suddenly and unexpectedly for no obvious reason.

When your child dies

The experts say that when a child dies, at whatever age and for whatever reason, the parents and those closest to them will suffer physical pain. This is not in your head. Your heart may literally be aching. And you are bound to suffer from other physical symptoms too, among them insomnia, a sensation of extreme exhaustion, the loss of memory and appetite and, often, the feeling that at any moment you will awaken from this devastating nightmare and discover the child you see over the heads of others in a crowded place is *your* child. Additionally, you may feel:

- Tightness in the chest and throat, or feelings of a lump in your stomach.
- Emptiness.
- Deep depression.
- A feeling of shortness of breath, excessive yawning, gasping for air, hyperventilating.
- A deep need to tell and retell and remember things about the child and the experience of its death.
- The uncontrollable act of bursting into tears at inappropriate moments and for no apparent reason.
- A loss of memory and a sudden discovery that you are wandering aimlessly: you may forget what you were saying mid-sentence, neglect to finish tasks, look for something to do and then find you are unable to concentrate long enough to do it.
- Feelings of intense anxiety.

Worst of all is the enormous, gaping chasm in your life and in your soul where your child ought to be.

This is all *normal*. It has been said that the bereaved underestimate their ability to survive. In any circumstances, and whoever's death you must live with, this is true. However, you *do* regain your health, your mind and your balance – through understanding your grief and working through it in your own way. You need the space and the time to heal in *your* way. You will never forget, nor would anyone expect you to. You do learn to live through it.

As people find it hard to find words of comfort for anyone suffering a bereavement, it is doubly difficult if there is a child involved, whether this is a miscarried baby, a stillborn infant, a toddler, teenager or adult. All that most of us can offer is outstretched arms to comfort, a cuddle, warmth and an open ear. Offers to help with practicalities and with other children in the family and with other responsibilities may be offered with love when outsiders don't know what else to do for you in the face of such tragedy. If you are the bereaved parents:

- DO try to talk to one another about what has happened. If you are a single parent, talk to your parents and your close friends.
- REMEMBER that a father's loss is every bit as devastating as the mother's. 'My wife was being treated as having lost someone she loved. I was being treated as having lost someone I was responsible for. I felt like shouting: "I loved him too, you know!",' one bereaved father told the Foundation for the Study of Infant Death.
- DO talk to any brothers or sisters, no matter how small they are, and try to explain that their sibling isn't coming back in terms that they are able to understand. (I go into more detail about how to help a child who has been bereaved in the next chapter.)
- DO ask professionals to explain to you exactly what has happened. This was your child, and you have every right to know all the details of their death if that is what you want.
- DO hold and cuddle your dead baby or child for as long as you

want to. Don't be hassled to hand over to the professionals until YOU are ready.

- DO choose the clothes you would like your child to be dressed in for the last time.
- DO accept any professional help that is offered.
- DO talk about your child openly in front of strangers. If they are embarrassed by this, that is their problem.
- DON'T let anyone try to tell you what to do or how to do it. Everyone grieves in their own way.

Photographs

DO take photographs of your baby or child, especially if your child died as a result of a stillbirth or a cot-death, where you may not have any other pictorial memories of the way she/he looked. You may not be able to look at them initially but later they will become very precious.

Photographs, whether of a stillborn or very young baby, a toddler or an older child throughout its life are vitally important to grieving parents and other family members, both at the time of death and through the years ahead according to all the parents to whom I have spoken in the course of researching this chapter. Photographs help keep the memories of their dead children fresh. It may seem almost macabre to think of taking a photograph of a child who never lived. However hard it may be, parents say they get enormous comfort from washing and dressing their baby and then posing the baby for a photograph to remember them by. The greatest need at the time of bereavement is to DO something. For parents whose hearts are broken and whose arms are aching, this may be the only thing they can ever do for their baby, other than bury it.

'Parents need to have mementoes to begin to help them have a focus for their grief and photographs are particularly important for parents who have little other evidence of their child's life,' advise the Child Bereavement Trust (Aston House, High Street, West Wycombe, Buckinghamshire HP14 3AG; telephone: 01494 446648; website: www.childbereavement.org.uk). 'All hospitals should have cameras which are capable of taking good, clear pictures. The way the pictures are taken is very important. It is important that the parents are given a choice about what clothes their baby is dressed in, and that there is a soft-coloured background. Most parents want to see as much of their baby as possible in some detail.'

The need for photographs of their dead brother or sister may later be incredibly important to brothers and sisters. Ann Deri-Bowen, National Co-ordinator of the Foundation for the Study of Infant Death herself had a two-month-old daughter, Nicola, who died a cot death. 'My daughter Nicola died in 1973 and at that time, all babies were put to sleep on their tummies,' she says. 'She hadn't been well and had spent two nights under observation in Odstock Hospital in Salisbury, but they had been unable to find anything wrong with her. Eight days later, I took her and my other daughter, then aged two, to have a cup of coffee with my husband's manager's wife who was a nurse. Nicola was in her pram which I had taken up to the bedroom. I checked on her and went downstairs for my coffee. I went back up about forty-five minutes later – and she was dead.

'Fortunately, we had taken a few photographs of her during her short life. One with each of the grandparents, one with me, her mum, one with her dad, one in the crib, one of her in her bouncy chair and one with her sister Sarah. These were so precious when they came back from the developers and went into an album. And there they stayed. I hadn't thought of having one on the wall or around the house.

'One day, many years later, when Sarah was sixteen, we were walking around the supermarket and she put some things in the basket. When we got to the checkout, I suggested she should pay for them herself. She opened her purse and to my surprise she showed me a photograph of Nicola in her bouncy chair which she had taken out of the album. She had suddenly felt the need to have the photograph of her sister with her. It really brought home to me that the photographs in the album were for all the family and that the value of having them there was something I couldn't begin to know. I was just so pleased that they were accessible and that Sarah had felt she could take one.'

Grandparents

People who have lost children have told me that when a child dies, and whatever the reason for the death, they feel isolated, devastated, and as though they are functioning in a 'fog', observing this terrible tragedy from outside as though it is happening to others. Most mothers and fathers who experience the death of their babies and children say that they cannot describe the pain they feel because it is the most intense of agonies and they wonder how on earth they can ever survive. They feel no one else can have any idea of what it feels like and how they never believed, at that time, that they could ever feel life would have a meaning again.

In the awareness of this life-shattering event which has devastated you, DON'T, please DON'T push grandparents away. They will be grieving too and may be unable to tell you how heartbroken they are for fear of making your anguish even more unbearable than it already is.

Tilly and Jeff, whose little grandson Jonny died tragically and suddenly at the age of just two, were devastated by his death even though they had four other grandchildren, three boys and a little girl. 'I have suffered from Parkinson's for years,' Jeff says. 'How can God have taken this lovely little boy when I could have gone instead? My life is over. His has hardly begun. I can't comfort my son and daughter-in-law. I don't know what to say and whatever I say seems wrong. They won't let me near their emotions. Nor do they understand how guilty we feel for being alive, me especially. I wish I could die and give them back their baby. It's not fair.'

At times, as with any other death, you may have to take the lead and let the grandparents know it's all right to talk about the dead child and to cry with you and for you. Neither Tilly nor Jeff committed the 'cardinal sin' of telling their children that they were young enough to have another baby. Sometimes, grandparents in particular, may say idiotic-sounding things just because it gives them additional torment to watch you, *their* child, going through such a horrendous trauma. If your child was very sick and they say 'Maybe it was all for the best' or 'At least you are young enough to have another one' forgive them! You may not believe that anyone can feel as anguished as you, but grandparents suffering not only for the lost and wasted young life but also for the raw pain they can see *their* children experiencing may be almost equally devastated.

Sue, whose son Jo died at the age of fourteen as a result of a rare, terminal disease, says: 'My husband died just eight months before Jo. I was facing caring for a profoundly disabled child alone. I also had a nine-year-old daughter.

'After my husband's sudden death, I had been terribly concerned about how I was going to cope with caring for Jo on a practical level. When he died, my immediate reaction was: "He's at peace and I won't have to struggle to cope alone any more." It was as though my husband had put out his arms and said: "You're not alone. I'll care for him now." It was such a relief not to worry about how I was going to get the Council to pay to install a downstairs toilet for Jo. Or about how I was going to do things with my daughter as Jo became progressively sicker. But, then my mother put into words what I had been feeling, and I was furious. I was so hurt and so angry with her because however handicapped Jo was, he was my son and I loved him and missed him. What I could say no one else could, not even my mother.' But, like everyone else, grandparents may find it as hard to find the right words to offer their bereaved children as strangers do. It is beyond their limited experience.

Writing out your feelings

Sometimes, there are things you can't say but that gnaw away at the very hem of your soul. There are so many things that you may have wanted to tell your child who is no longer within reach or hearing. There may be apologies you want to make for the 'telling-off' you gave them unjustly when you thought they were naughty. There may be praise and pride which you felt, but never found time to give or express. There may be feelings you never expressed for fear of being thought silly, stupid or embarrassing. There may be things so private that you cannot voice them, even to those who are closest to you, but which you can release by writing them down.

If you are feeling weighed down by things you just need to unburden, you might consider keeping a 'feelings' diary. Buy a small notebook and keep it with you all the time so that you can write things down as they pop into your head. Re-reading these feelings can feel very soothing.

Sharing experiences

If your child was sick, then it is more than likely that you will have been involved with a group of parents with similarly sick children before their death. If your child died suddenly, either as a result of an illness or foul play, there are any number of organisations set up by people who have suffered similar experiences and who may be ready and willing to offer you help. Don't knock it! They say that a trouble shared is a trouble halved and it really is true that it helps to talk and interact with other people who have experienced what you are experiencing, who have felt and thought the often-violent emotions which must be racing round inside your head and who can empathise from a position of experience with how you feel.

Laurie Didham, the Development Officer for the Child Death Helpline, says: 'After the death of a child, particularly a sick or handicapped child, many parents who have devoted their entire lives to that child since birth or since the time the illness was diagnosed, don't know what to do with their lives. I have met people whose children have died and who tell me that they have spent the next sixteen years wondering what to do next. I believe the answer is to talk about it to professionals such as counsellors. Then, look for an organisation whose aims you care about and offer to help others who may be going through what you have been through.

'I started working at the Child Death Helpline as a volunteer after my own daughter, Rebecca, died thirteen years ago. Gradually, I became more and more involved. Now I am a paid member of staff and this is work I care passionately about because I've been there.'

Without in any way wishing to minimalise the chasm of emptiness the death of anyone, but most particularly a child, leaves, the death of a child leaves a void in activity. From organising your life around your child and its needs, suddenly there is nothing to do for that child any more. Or is there?

Many parents, like Gail and Harry Moore, find that doing something in their dead child's memory not only helps soothe their own pain, but may offer some help to others suffering similarly.

Gail and Harry's daughter Laura and her twin brother Kit, the couple's first children, were born in Leicester in 1985. Laura was first diagnosed with acute leukaemia in 1988, aged two years and eleven months. She was treated at Leicester Royal Infirmary, where she was on an adult ward. The medical care she received was, say her parents, of the finest. However, their baby girl was with much older people as she battled against her disease.

'We longed for her to be among other children and not in a hospital atmosphere,' Harry explains. Then we saw a TV programme called: *A Place for Tom*. It was about a centre that had been set up in Liverpool to offer help and support to parents of terminally sick children with cancer and we thought: 'That's what we need in Leicester.'

After a hard-fought battle, Laura died on 28 January 1990. 'We were all struck by grief,' says Harry. 'One day Gail would be down and the next day it would be me. I think it's often easier for fathers. They have work to occupy them during the day. Nor did we realise how much children grieve for their siblings. Kit and Laura were five when Laura died. There were times when we could see Kit's emptiness and we despaired of ways to help him.'

By the time of Laura's death, the Moores had had another little son, Adam, who was twelve months at the time of his sister's death. Georgina, their youngest daughter, is now eight. She has grown up always knowing that she once had a sister called Laura. 'We tell her: "You are Laura's only sister. Laura was poorly and she died." But Laura is still a living part of Kit, Georgina and Adam's lives in another, very practical way.

'After her death, we were approached by Rainbows, a children's respite centre in Leicester which provides family-centred respite care for children with life-threatening or life-limiting illness,' Harry explains. 'They knew we were interested in child death and in doing more to help other parents. So we put our thinking caps on and set about raising money for 'The Laura Centre' – where other bereaved parents can find help. As a family, we raised half-a-million pounds. The Prince of Wales came to open the centre where seven or eight professional counsellors are available to counsel bereaved parents like us. We are very proud of what we have achieved in Laura's name.'

If you have a problem finding an organisation that is pertinent to you, you might seek one out in a book such as *The Voluntary Agencies Directory* published by Barclays, a copy of which is bound to be found in your local library.

Many, if not all, of these organisations originated when the parents of sick children banded together, or when those whose children have died determined that their children would not have died for nothing. If they could do no more to help their own youngsters, then they determined to help others and, by so-doing, would keep the memory of their own children fresh and alive.

Attending meetings with other bereaved parents, wherever you are, is not just a way of reliving the death of your child. Although most parents feel isolated in the beginning, the group helps them to know they haven't been singled out for this unspeakable hurt. Healing does happen through sharing.

Mums and dads – different attitudes to the death of your child

Mothers and fathers do grieve in different ways. While mothers yearn to talk about the child who has died, and will share their thoughts and feelings openly (sometimes relentlessly!) with other members of their families and their closest friends, men generally try to hide their feelings and preserve the 'stiff upper lip' associated with true Brits. They will hold it all in rather than risk upsetting their wives.

Men who are grieving for their children will often:

- Insist that a child's bedroom is locked and nothing touched after the death, sometimes leaving it exactly as it was for many years.
- Ban the child's friends from visiting the house, even when the mother thinks it will give her comfort.
- Refuse to join self-help groups or mix socially with old friends.
- Throw themselves into their jobs.

Women who are grieving for their children will often:

- Seek out the company of any other woman prepared to listen to them talking about their child.
- Keep something belonging to the child close to them at all times – it may be a small toy, a nappy or, with an older child, a piece of jewellery.
- Join self-help groups and seek out others in the same situation to whom they can relate easily.

Both parents may make 'martyrs' of their dead children and this can be dangerous if there are other children in the family who are grieving too. It may leave these young survivors feeling that they can never quite measure up to their 'perfect' dead brothers or sisters, that the 'favourite' has died, and that they will only ever be second best, no matter how hard they try (so often they see no point in bothering and their rebellious behaviour can cause even more trauma within the family). *Never* tell a sibling that their dead brother or sister would never have done/behaved/acted-up the way they are doing. The truth is, you will never know!

Talking to one another

When things are so at odds, your relationship with your partner can be stretched beyond the limit. It's very hard to talk about something that hurts so much – but parents who made a child together should talk about it together after its death. It's not easy to let the barriers down, most especially to your nearest and dearest. The temptation to tread egg-shells for fear of adding to the anguish is compelling. But what you fear may cause your partner extra pain may also be a method of driving a wedge between you as a couple. Any subject that is taboo is a subject that needs to be aired in any relationship. Treading egg-shells in the face of a child's death is something that you need to resist – and it's something that grandparents should resist too.

Phillip, who lost his son Owen sixteen years ago, says: 'We walked on egg-shells with one another for a long time. In the initial period, especially, we both felt we had to be careful not to precipitate floods of tears from each other.

'I was at work and I'd go out on my own at lunch time and walk along the Embankment and cry my eyes out. Then I'd dry my tears, put myself back together and return to the office as though nothing had happened. That way, I didn't need to cry in front of my wife. Perhaps I should have done. We tried not to burst into tears in front of one another, even if we were feeling really awful. We both struggled to keep our balance. But then we'd try to make little jokes about things Owen had said or done and then end up weeping in one another's arms. I would advise others not to seek to find jokes about the dead child, certainly not at the beginning. We tried to remind ourselves about how good life had been with Owen and recall the funny things he'd said and done but it certainly didn't work for us.'

Physical contact with a partner – and others

The Foundation for the Study of Infant Death explains that while one of you may yearn for physical contact, the other may shun it. This applies to the death of any child, not just a baby. One partner may be frightened that the other 'wants to make another baby to replace the one who is lost' when all they really want is a cuddle and solace and reassurance that their partner isn't 'blaming' them for the death. Or, they may feel that cuddling their partner will in some way lessen the suffering they need to feel in the wake of this tragedy.

It is as though they are punishing themselves. It may well be worth the whole family spending time together as a unit once the funeral is over, perhaps adopting the format of the Jewish custom of shiva, and permitting themselves a week or two when they stay at home together with the closest members of the family and let it be known that visitors are welcome to come and talk about the child who has died. Such a 'time out' tactic can also ease the path for the time ahead, when bereaved parents, like any other who grieves, want to be treated as normal rather than set apart as the parents who suffered that 'dreadful tragedy'.

Other people's reactions

As with any other death, people have no idea what to say, if anything at all, when they meet you after the death of a child. You can cut their embarrassment with a knife and although they may be well meaning, they cannot comprehend the depth of your grief:

- Some will say nothing at all.
- Some will avoid you.
- Some will face you, but will attempt to keep off the subject of your child.
- Some will refuse to answer questions about their own children for fear of upsetting you.
- Some may feel very vulnerable and, for this reason, they may fail to keep up friendships.

You can take the lead

If someone says: 'You'll get over it' or 'You can have another one', tell them that those are not terms that you wish to talk in. In these circumstances, there's no etiquette about being blunt and someone who truly cares will understand and, hopefully, apologise.

If you are asked by a stranger how many children you have, include the dead child in your family count – and then tell them that one died. It is perfectly fine to acknowledge that your child existed and that you know what it is like to be a parent.

Of course it is going to hurt when you meet other people who have children of a similar age to that of the child who has died. You cannot avoid meeting them, unless you plan to hide yourself away for the rest of your life and you can't do that.

Phillip says: 'My only child Owen was eighteen when he died as the result of a cycle crash which was his own fault. Many of his friends from the church have kept in touch with us over the years and now they invite us to their weddings and their children's christenings. When one of Owen's closest school friends married recently, my wife Sandra and I were invited to the wedding. You feel quite sad at moments because you realise that someone is missing. That we're at this wedding instead of him. There are blips because such feelings do hit your emotions. Then you think you are there to celebrate the happiness of one of his friends. One challenging moment came during the course of the speeches. Something was said that reminded us of Owen. A sheer pain went through us both. But then we thought: "This is not the time or the place to be in floods of tears. It is a time for pleasure." Perhaps the thing that is most painful to us is when people go on and on about their grandchildren. Little babies are lovely and we enjoy hearing how our friends' grandchildren are growing up. We ask all the right polite questions. What we can't bear is "grandchildren bores". We know we'll never have any of our own.'

Laurie Didham says: 'Even though it's many years since our baby daughter Rebecca died, someone said the other day that I'm 'lucky' because now I'll only have to go through the teenage tantrums syndrome once. It was said in all innocence, but to someone who has lost a child, it is mortifying and stupid, and it has made me angry in a way I haven't felt in years. I think to myself even now how much I would love to have to deal with two sets of teenage tantrums.'

An only child

If you have lost your only child, you may feel desperately sad that now, in the eyes of the outside world, you are a childless family. If, like Sandra and Phillip, you lose an only child and are too old to have any more children – or perhaps don't want any more – this may be an additional bereavement. When in future you're asked whether you have a family, never be scared to say: 'I did have a child but she/ he died.' You were a parent and a good one at that. You know what it is like to have children and you don't begrudge other people their happiness and their shared family lives, although there will be times when it hurts to see families, particularly families with children the age of your dead child, together.

There are a number of excellent organisations to which you can turn for expert help following the death of a child, and this applies whether you have family support or not. Indeed, some of the organisations involved offer advice and support for other members of the family, too, including brothers and sisters, grandparents and others who may have been closely affected by the death – such as teachers and even health-care professionals.

In the UK you will find:
- The Child Bereavement Trust is a charity which cares for grieving families by training and supporting professional carers. They produce resources to help both adults and children who are grieving. Although they do not have a helpline of their own, they provide some excellent literature and companion books and videos such as *When our Baby Died*, a video for bereaved parents which is accompanied by a book called *Grieving After the Death of Your Baby* which has been praised by Dr Colin Murray Parkes of Bereavement Care, and by CRUSE as 'a remarkably interesting and sensitive video that will be of great help to parents who have lost a baby'. They also hold specialist information to help parents grieving for a child with a disability, to help children with grief after the death of a brother or sister, and to help those facing infertility treatment which, they say, covers the grief of

not conceiving naturally. They also produce items such as the Memory Box and Wallet which can prove very helpful to both grieving parents and children.

- The Child Death Helpline is staffed by bereaved parent volunteers who are supported by a professional team. This is NOT a counselling service but provides a 'listening' service for those affected by the death of a child and the chance to talk to someone else who has also been affected by such a death. It will allow you to recognise, acknowledge and cope with all the powerful emotions and frightening feelings that losing a child engenders. It will help you learn to live with the long-term nature and the sadness of grief and someone will be there to advise you at the hardest times such as birthdays, anniversaries, milestones and family events.

- The Foundation for the Study of Infant Death (FSID) was set up to prevent unexpected deaths in infancy and promote infant help. They not only fund research, they offer support, including befriending support, to families whose babies have died suddenly and unexpectedly; publish information about cot death for health-care professionals and parents, brothers, sisters and other family members; and, although the organisation is totally areligious, it sponsors religious services of remembrance to commemorate the lives of the babies who have died around Christmas time. They have also set into place a scheme known as CONI (Care of the Next Infant). This means that parents who have had a baby die suddenly and unexpectedly, and who later go on to have subsequent babies, are now supported by specially trained health professionals in 90 per cent of the country.

- The Compassionate Friends offer help and consolation to all members of a bereaved family and although they are Bristol-based, they have groups countrywide. They are to be found at 53 North Street, Bristol BS1 3EN and their helpline, 0117 953 9639, is manned seven days a week. They will be able to find befrienders who have been through the experience and will talk to you over the phone.

These befrienders are not counsellors but people who have been through the experience themselves and who have undertaken a training programme to help them help you. They will listen if you need an ear; support the whole family when it needs support most; publish newsletters, leaflets, booklets and books; and run a postal library service with specialist books on the loss of children of any age. Sheila, who works as a volunteer for Compassionate Friends, and who often mans their helpline says: 'Parents, most particularly mothers, often get on the phone and, when I say: "Tell me about it", the floodgates open and all their emotions pour out. They need reassurance that these overwhelming and powerful emotions are normal. They say they can't think straight. They complain they can't concentrate. They tell me they are so forgetful that they go to make a cup of tea and can't remember what they are doing with a kettle in their hands. You have to keep telling them: "It's OK. You are not going mad. This is how it is after a child dies." The one thing we don't do on the phone is make suggestions. But we will invite people to join – joining Compassionate Friends costs £28 a year which is just to cover the cost of the regular newsletter – and we invite them to local meetings which are run by bereaved parents, generally in someone's home or a local church hall. When you go along to a group, you need have no fear that you will be expected to tell your story. No one is expected to say anything until they want to and they feel ready.'

- CRUSE offer counselling and literature for anyone who has been bereaved, whatever their relationship to the deceased and this includes specialist literature aimed at those who have lost children.
- The Association of Children's Hospices offers the parents and other relatives concerned with the care and welfare of life-limited children support and practical help throughout the lives of their children and counselling and help after their death. They can advise on hospices countrywide. Contact them at Kings House, 14 Orchard Street, Bristol BS1 5EH, or telephone them

on 01179 055082. Visit their website at www.childhospice.
org.uk for further information.

- ACT (Association for Children with Life Threatening or
Terminal Conditions and their Families) is a Bristol-based
organisation which provides a national information resource for
parents and key workers caring for children with life threatening
or terminal conditions. They publish a comprehensive pack
on the children's hospice movement. Their address is Orchard
House, Orchard Lane, Bristol BS1 5DT and their telephone
number is 0117 930 4707.

- The Acorns Children's Hospice Trust offers emotional and
practical support, and increases awareness and information about
the plight of life-limited children and their families. They suggest
that anyone needing support should contact Acorns, 103 Oak
Tree Lane, Sellyoak, Birmingham B29 6HZ, or telephone 0121
248 4850. They are based predominantly in the West Midlands
Health Authority region and north Gloucestershire. Their work
extends, naturally, to counselling families through their child's
terminal illness and through bereavement. Visit their website at
www.acorns.org.uk.

There are many other local charities, attached to the hospice
movement and children's hospitals, which offer mutual help for
bereaved parents but they are too numerous to list here.

In the US there are:
- Bereaved Parents of the USA, PO Box 95, Park Forest, Illinois
60466, offers self-help similar to the British Compassionate
Friends. They, too, are interdenominational and offer newsletters
and the opportunity to meet up with other bereaved parents
locally through self-help groups which are nationwide. You can
visit their website at www.bereavedparentsusa.org for further
details. Members are at all stages of recovery and some have deep
religious faith, while others have lost their faith, and still others
are adrift. Attendance at the meetings brings together newly
bereaved parents and those who are further along in their grief

and have worked through many of their grief-related issues.

- The Children's Hospice International in Alexandria, Virginia was inaugurated in 1977 after an eight-year-old boy was denied hospice support because he was a child. This denial triggered the crusade for children's hospice care and the official development of CHI. Initially, only four hospice programmes in the United States would accept children. CHI has worked effectively to dramatically change these numbers. Today, almost all hospice programmes in the US are willing to consider accepting a child as a patient.

  The CHI works closely with medical professionals as a research and resource bank, providing technical assistance, research and education. They can be reached at 901 North Pitt Street, Suite 230, Alexandria, VA22314. Their telephone number is (001) 703 684 0030. You can visit their website at www.chionline.org for further information.

Befrienders

You may not feel that you want or need face-to-face counselling, particularly at the very beginning when you are surrounded by family and friends. But sometimes, talking to a total stranger over the phone, particularly one who understands the anguish you are suffering because they have suffered such agony themselves, can be a comfort. You may gain a great deal of comfort by speaking to a stranger you can't see and will never meet but who can listen, sympathise and remain non-judgemental. Many of the above organisations offer excellent befriending services. Not only will befrienders have first-hand experience, but they are trained and supervised. Contact individual organisations for further details.

7

When children are bereaved

A century ago, most people died at home. Death and grieving were a part of family life accepted by each member of the family – including the children.

However, as medical care improved, so the subject of death became taboo, especially where children were concerned. Fifty years ago, death was not a subject to be discussed with children, even if the children themselves were bereaved. They didn't need to know the details. How do I know? Because I was one of those children who was 'protected' from death – and it took me well into adulthood to come to terms with what had happened.

My mother died when I was three years old, as I explained at the beginning of this book. I have no memory of what I was told at the time although presumably someone must have said something to explain the absence of the lady with the brown hair who was always in bed. My only memory is that when I was very good, she gave me green sweets covered in sugar from a brown-paper bag she kept by her bed, just for me. Then she wasn't there – and then she was! My father remarried six months later and I thought my new mummy was the old one, come back to take care of me again. I tried very hard to be good so she wouldn't go away again. I have memories of a few strange things, which concerned my grandparents who were not allowed to see me any more for reasons I don't need to explain here. However, no mention was ever made of my original mother again, until I was seven years old when a friend taunted me: 'Ha! Ha! You haven't got a mummy and I have! She's not your mummy!'

The old-fashioned view was that children are resilient – they would 'bounce back' and they were too young to understand or know differently, especially if they were under four. They could be spared the details and, in my case at least, this was a subject never to be discussed. I had a mother and whether she was the woman who had given birth to me was immaterial. Today, those who advise bereaved parents and children know better.

Now it is accepted that children bereaved by the death of parents or siblings need expert help to support them through their bereavement, even if they are only babies or toddlers at the time of the death and seemingly have little understanding of what has happened. They need to be told the whole truth, and they need to know of their origins just as adopted children do. It helps to have some kind of 'life-book' in which the part in their lives played by the person who has died can be seen and returned to whenever they choose.

If children don't get the help they need at the time they need it, if they are denied the basic right to grieve, whether because they are being 'protected' from death by over-zealous adults (as I was), because their emotions are thought to be of little consequence at such an early age, or because it is felt that the true basic facts of what has happened are more than they will be able to bear, it is now known they may get stuck in a rut of grief. This can have a profound effect on their emotions, their mental stability and their perception of the world later in life. Yet, helping a child through bereavement can be a dreadful additional burden if you are grieving too.

When somebody within the family is very ill and death is expected, it is only fair, and only sensible, to try to prepare them for what is about to happen. What they need is intelligent guidance and proper answers to the questions they will inevitably ask in language they can understand and which is appropriate to their age.

If a parent is dying, the other healthy parent may find this an ominous task, but parents to whom I have spoken and who found themselves in this situation said they found it was actually a relief to tell their children what was going on.

'My daughters were aged seven and nine when their daddy was dying,' says Pat, whose husband Jeremy died of cancer in a hospice when he was 43 years old. 'My older daughter wanted to spend time sitting holding her daddy's hand and I let her. The hospice said I should let both of them do whatever they wanted to. He was kept relatively pain-free and she was old enough to tell him all her news, which amused both of them, and to hold his hand. My little daughter didn't like seeing her daddy being in bed all day. I took her along several times and she just kept tugging his hand and saying: "Get up, Daddy. Please get up and come home." She was very upset by it all so I used to take the older girl and leave the younger one to play with her friends. When Jeremy died, I explained that he had gone to heaven and was living with God up on his own cloud. I told the little one that he was able to walk around again and he didn't have any pain and was much better. She accepted that. Even now, she's a teenager but she often talks about her daddy on his "little cloud".'

If you can't talk about the dying person to your child, ask someone else who knows them well to help prepare them for what's happening. It may well be that an aunt or uncle or close friend will help and will know how the child finds it easiest to express themselves. Very small children may find it easier to show their feelings through drawing, painting and colours.

It may be music or poetry that can catch the right note. If a pet has died, it can be helpful to recall how sad everyone was and what happened. Under-eights are often very interested in the whole concept of death, but may find it hard to grasp its finality. They may have their own ideas about how life continues after death or how people come back to life again – and this may be compounded by their teaching and understanding of religion. Jesus rose again, so why shouldn't their parent or brother or sister?

Many very young children, like Pat's daughter, accept that the person who has died has gone to live with God – or that they are now the brightest star in the sky. By making this preparation part of everyday life, death will become a natural thing. Talking about the death of a pet – or even the death of a flower or plant may offer the opening a child needs to discuss death.

Sudden death is a different scenario. When someone has died as a result of sudden, unexpected circumstances such as heart failure, stroke, accident, terrorist attack or murder it is hard enough for adults to grasp, let alone children. Of course, there can be no preparation for death in such circumstances.

According to Dr Dorothy Judd, a child psychotherapist who works with The Child Psychotherapy Trust in London, The Trust specialises in helping children of all ages, from babies to older teenagers, come to terms with the death of loved ones. It is perfectly normal for young children to think about death, just as they think about their bodies, sex and life.

'Although adults may find it difficult to talk about death due to their own anxieties about their mortality or fear of upsetting others, it is important *not* to assume that children are not ready and willing to talk about their anxieties on the subject.

'Indeed, this can be the most useful way in which parents and other important adults in their lives, such as teachers, nurses and GPs, can help children cope with bereavement. Being prepared to *listen* to the child's thoughts, beliefs and fears about death is the first step,' she says. 'By listening, the adult shows that he or she is strong enough to cope with whatever it is the child wants to talk about. Of course, children respond differently at different ages and their reactions are hard for parents to comprehend. Children tend to slip in and slip out of grief in a way that can be shocking and upsetting to a grieving adult.'

Dr Judd says that children have different responses to death and dying, depending on their age and experience. There are no clear-cut stages, she says, as to a correct order or a prescribed duration of grieving but she suggests it may help to know some fairly typical stages you may see.

Where very young children, and even babies, are concerned, and they are too young to have language to express their feelings, don't underestimate their loss: even the very youngest children and babies will be aware that people they were attached to have gone, and experience the dawning realisation that they are never coming back and that death is permanent.

'Babies and young children cry heartbrokenly when they feel unsafe – if, for example a parent leaves the room in ordinary circumstances, leaving them in the care of a babysitter. However, after a death, and when the loved one doesn't come back at all, they can feel scared about their own survival. For those who cannot speak, there is no name for this dread. They may be comforted by adults but when those adults are too devastated themselves to offer comfort, it is vital to try to arrange for a carer to take over in a loving and safe environment where they can see those they love who remain alive regularly. Because a death in the family affects everyone, there will be disruption. Make no mistake. It will leave a scar – as death scars us all. But, as the child grows up, it is important to talk about the person who has died and explain what has happened. It is vital for the child and those caring for them to keep memories of the dead person alive.'

Signs that children are grieving:

- They may feel numbness and disbelief, just as adults do. Comfort them. Cuddle them. Reassure them that *you* are not going to leave them for a very long time. But just as adults sometimes don't want to discuss death, so children may not want to talk at times. Let them talk about it when, and as, they want to. *Don't force them to talk*. And don't be surprised, shocked or feel they are 'heartless' if they talk about death one moment and go out to play football the next. That is the normal, natural way.
- Like you, a child may be deeply shocked by what has happened and depressed at the loss. Sleep disturbance is natural. Just comfort and cuddle as needed. They will need lots of attention.
- They may behave too well because they're scared that their 'bad' behaviour is in some way responsible for the death of the person they love. Children may feel very guilty that they have 'caused' the death, just by thinking or wishing the person who has died

would go away at one time or another. They need to be reassured time and time again that they are absolutely in no way responsible for the death and that they cannot, possibly be to blame.

- Many children deny what has happened. Denial is a necessary anaesthetic. In time, says Dr Judd, the reality will find its way through their self-protection. There's no need to constantly reiterate the truth. Going to the funeral and cemetery can be helpful. Funerals don't have to be sad or unpleasant and many children will choose to go if they understand that this is the time to bid a final farewell to someone they love. Try to explain in advance what is going to happen.

Funerals – take the children or leave them at home?

Final goodbyes are as important for children as they are for adults. Denying a child the right to bid a proper farewell to someone they love dearly will make it far harder for them to accept the situation. A funeral is a ceremony that helps a child accept death. The child in a family that has suffered a bereavement has the same rights as every other member of that family to 'close the circle' of life by being there *if that is their choice.*

However, they need to understand exactly what a funeral or cremation is; what they will see and what they won't see. Above all, they need to be reassured that the person inside the coffin isn't able to feel anything of what is happening around them, or feel any pain. Whether the child decides to go to the funeral or not, make sure they understand exactly what is going to happen. Explain that everyone who is there will be feeling very sad because they loved Granny, Grandpa, Mummy, Daddy or the sister or brother who has died. You can say that people may cry – and that if they want to cry then that is OK. If the grief of the people closest to the child, such as the parents, is so overwhelming that they can't bring themselves to take over the explanations themselves, then a trusted relative or family friend should be asked to take on this vital task.

Children may ask if they can go to a religious service or first part of the funeral but not to the burial or cremation, and that can usually be arranged. Encourage them to talk about their feelings but leave the final decision to the child.

Laurie Didham explains: 'We told Elizabeth before the funeral that Becky's body would be in a little white box and for a child who is barely three that it is a hard concept to grasp. I remember she asked would she be able to look in and we said she couldn't because there would be too many people there. She just seemed to accept that. In a way that's easy because very few children of that age challenge it. An older child might. A lot of people said we were wrong to let Elizabeth go to Becky's funeral. She was the only child there. We felt it was right that she should say goodbye to her sister with us. We are a united family and we needed to be a family more than at any other time on that day.'

Children often behave with greater dignity than we credit them with having. Anyone who witnessed the demeanour of Princes William and Harry at the funeral of their mother, the late Princess Diana, will recall the enormous dignity of those two young teenagers as they marched upright behind their mother's coffin which bore a white wreath with the simple word 'Mummy'. If a child is old enough, let them pay their respects in their own words and in their own way, and write their own words on any wreath or death announcement to be placed in the local paper.

Siblings

As I mentioned in the last chapter, it is vital not to 'deify' a dead sibling to the surviving brothers and sisters. It is hard enough to comprehend that the other young person who shared their parents, their home and their life isn't coming back, ever. There will be no more fighting over who watches what on TV. No more squabbling over who sits in the armchair or who gets the last cake, or who started the fight.

It may be very hard for parents to do, but when there are other children in a household, don't build shrines and start to hold up the one who has died as a perfect and ideal child to whom no one and nothing can ever measure successfully. The child's siblings will be left feeling that 'the wrong child' died – or that they can only ever be 'second best' in their parents' eyes. The result can be low self-esteem and lead to all kinds of other problems later in life. Have photographs around of the dead child. Keep treasures. But talk about the dead child as a normal child who could be very good or very naughty. Laugh at the naughty memories with the surviving children and it will help you cope, too.

Helen and Neil

It isn't always possible to break the news of a loved one's death to a child yourself. When Helen and Neil's baby son Thomas died last year at the age of eleven weeks as a result of Cot Death syndrome, the whole family were in a state of shock.

'It all happened so quickly,' Helen said. 'I went in to feed him in the morning and he was laying in his cot, cold. I picked him up and tried mouth-to-mouth resuscitation. But he'd gone. We called an ambulance. They came. The police came. It is all a blur now. We spent the whole day crying, hugging one another and trying to understand. Our little boy, Joseph, then aged four, was bewildered. I felt I should tell him what had happened but I couldn't find the words. In the end, a wonderful policewoman took over. She took Joseph outside and told him to look up in the sky at night-time and when he saw the brightest star in the sky, he would know that was Thomas.

'That thought not only gives Joseph comfort. It gives me comfort too. Joseph will suddenly say: "Look, Mummy. There's the Thomas star. Wave to him. He is following us." I think that is really sweet. It makes me feel that he really is with us.'

Explaining death

Trying to explain death to a child, particularly a very young child, is never easy. However, the following guidelines may be helpful:

- Use straightforward words like 'dead' and 'dying'. Try to link these words to circumstances the child has experienced such as the death of a pet (which may have caused the child more grief than any parent or guardian could anticipate).

- Avoid saying: 'Daddy's gone to sleep' or 'Mummy's gone away' or 'We lost Grandma' because these concepts can be confused with everyday living experiences and may lead to great fears of going to sleep or getting lost. It is better to explain that the body has not 'gone' anywhere except into a box to the cemetery or crematorium.

- Children do often confuse death and sleep, particularly those under the age of four, but older children may also feel that the two are linked. You will need to explain the difference by saying something like: 'When you are asleep, your body works very well and is busy growing and healing all the scratches you got during the day. When you wake up after a good sleep, you feel really good and full of energy. When someone dies, it means his or her body is no longer working at all. You may be able to explain that they were feeling very sore, but now that their bodies don't work any longer, they can't feel any more pain. Explain that being a person is more than just having a body. It means having a soul, and you can explain what happens to the soul within the context of your religion, saying that perhaps he or she is now living with God or Jesus and is looking down on them from heaven.

- Sometimes children ask to see a body after death. It may be helpful to allow them to do so in order to help them understand what has happened.

- Tell the story of the death as easily as you can. Over the years, it may be necessary to repeat it again and again so that the child can get it all straight in their minds.

How you can deal with questions

Listen carefully when a child asks a question and answer as straightforwardly and as honestly as you can. Children ask direct questions which can sometimes make an adult feel very embarrassed. 'What is a coffin like inside?' 'If they put grandma in a box in the ground how will she get out?' 'Is it going to be lonely lying in a box all alone and is it dark and scary down there?' Such questions may make an adult feel very uncomfortable and children, who are very sensitive to such discomfort, may stop asking questions for fear of upsetting them. Remember that children have short attention spans. They will rush in from a game, ask the hardest question in the world, listen and absorb the answer and then demand to turn on their favourite TV programme.

Anger

Just as adults are angered by bereavement, so are children. The anger may manifest itself in many ways. Older children and adolescents may say: 'How could she/he have left me?' or 'Why couldn't the doctors make them better?' Acknowledging a child's anger and feeling of abandonment when you are feeling both angry and abandoned yourself may not be easy – especially when you are exhausted and struggling to cope with your own emotions but do give them permission to cry.

Someone told one of my daughters that she had to 'be strong for Mummy and mustn't cry', thus diminishing her own loss. I couldn't understand her apparent lack of emotion. I knew how much she adored her dad. It wasn't until long afterwards, when we were talking one day, that she told me why she hadn't cried and why she had apparently treated her father's death so 'lightly'. I could have strangled the well-meaning but misguided person who insisted that she should 'be strong' for me. She had her right to grief and mourning. Crying together was the best thing we ever did.

Reassure your children, give them permission to be sad, to cry, to mourn. Agree with the way they say they feel. Let them know they are not alone with their feelings. They may feel despairing. Just as you are feeling. Don't push a child away. Let them share your grief and show them that you want to share theirs. There is no way of taking away the grieving process, as much as you want to protect them. The best way you can help is to allow them to cry and grieve openly. Stored grief in a child can open a hornet's nest of misery in an adult's mind. Take it from one who knows!

Behaviour

If a child has been bereaved, no matter what their age, a significant death can leave them feeling terribly insecure. They may withdraw into a seemingly private existence. They may fail to show emotion and appear almost detached from the world, or they may become overwhelmed by apparently innocuous events. As such behaviour is part of normal adolescence, it may be hard to know what is normal and what is a reaction to the train of events.

The important thing is to let any bereaved child know you are there and that you are ready to offer them love and support at all times.

The teenage years

Of course, there is no 'good' time to lose someone important in your life. But, the teenage years are a particularly difficult time to experience the death of someone you love. As if it isn't bad enough having hormones rushing wildly round their bodies, upsetting emotions at the best and most stable of family times, coping with a major bereavement and the grief this involves on top of normal pressures can feel almost unbearably stressful.

As with adults, guilt is a major factor. The Child Bereavement Trust specialists say that a teenager may, perhaps, have been going through a bad patch in a relationship with the parent, brother or sister who has died, and it may almost feel to them as if they had 'wished' for the death and possessed more power than they believed possible.

Their security may be doubly threatened by their bereavement. If their father has died, and he was the breadwinner, they may be scared about who will now pay the bills. If it is their mother who has died, who will care for them, their home and the practicalities of everyday life? These thoughts and fears may be almost impossible to voice to other loved ones who are suffering from the same loss. Furthermore, how can friends who have never faced such trauma understand – particularly when they may not want to listen, and may find such discussion embarrassing? The Trust say it is vital to let a young person know that:

- It is OK to cry and feel low and depressed.
- It is OK to be angry, embarrassed and not want to talk about deep feelings.
- It is OK to live in the past for a while as a means of keeping the memory of the person who has died fresh and alive.
- It is OK to have fun and laugh. This will in no way degrade the memory of the person who has died.
- It is OK to forgive yourself for fights or arguments you may have had with the person who died and the nasty things you may have said to them.
- It is OK to go on living.

However, make it plain that it is NOT OK to:

- Act out frustrations by doing mad things or by skipping school.
- Experiment with drugs or alcohol to dull your senses and hide the pain.
- Experiment with casual sex just to get close to someone else.
- Do things in anger that will hurt other people because you are hurting yourself.
- Act as a scapegoat or bad person to look tough.

Sarah

Sarah's father died in a car accident when she was fifteen. In a moving *Teenage Guide to Coping with Bereavement* pamphlet that she wrote for The Child Bereavement Trust, Sarah says:

Angry things kept buzzing in my mind. When you're a teenager, just when everything's starting in your life then it is reduced to cinders suddenly. I felt guilty of this anger, and I just decided to continue and manage these big things at the same time. Then I felt I must protect my mother and brother because they needed me.

When someone close to you dies, you suddenly have a lot of difficult emotions to deal with. Whether the death was expected or not, you will still feel shock. After these first very confusing feelings, others will come which may surprise or even frighten you.

Sarah advises other young people who may find themselves in the situation she is in that while some people may be happy to go back to school quickly, others may prefer to have a little time to get themselves together. 'Don't feel guilty about having time off,' she advises other young people. 'Giving yourself extra hassle is pointless. Exams can be taken again, but your life can't. Remember, everyone is different, so do whatever feels right for you.' And, she advises, as time goes on, and if you feel you have no one to talk to, it's always possible to find a counsellor.

Amanda

Amanda Townsend, now twenty-eight, lost her identical-twin sister Deborah to bone cancer when they were fourteen. 'When you've been in the womb for nine months with someone and you share the same genes, there is a bond which is stronger than any other human relationship. When that disappears, it is devastating,' she said in an interview in the *Sunday Mirror* in September 1999.

'We would argue sometimes and had different hobbies but she was always there and I never imagined a time when she wouldn't be.'

Deborah was ill for about two years before her death. 'I don't think I ever believed she would actually die,' says Amanda. 'I remember feeling jealous at times when she got all the attention but she was so brave and unselfish and she managed to stay cheerful right up to the end.

'When she died, I felt completely numb. I don't remember what I did for the first six months but apparently I didn't cry a lot.

'I was angry and confused. I just buried myself in my school-work and studied all the time. That was my way of trying to shut out what had happened. The worst thing was the way other people treated me. They didn't know what to say and so would often avoid me altogether.'

Amanda admits that as time went on, she wondered why it was Deborah and not she who had died. 'I would have done anything to swap places with her,' she says.

The memory box

A 'memory box' can be very helpful for anyone who has been bereaved, but no more so than for a child who is desperate to 'hold on' to memories that may be fading fast. This is a place where they can keep small but deeply treasured memorabilia associated with their dead loved one – e.g. photographs, letters, poems. The focus given to remembering will be greatly valued as, this way, they will know that grieving is about remembering, not about forgetting. A child's memory box need not be a grand affair, but a special place, which they can make and decorate for themselves. Give them a notebook where there's space to write or draw about feelings through the years. Make sure that a bereaved child has their own, personal photograph of the person who has died which they can keep in whatever 'secret place' they choose. Even if your own circumstances change, perhaps if you remarry, never ever deprive them of their photograph or of their memory box.

Reassurance

It is absolutely vital that children know that they are NEVER responsible for the death of the person they have loved. They need to know that nothing they have ever thought or done could have caused it – and that there is nothing they could have done to prevent it.

It is absolutely vital that they are told, over and over, that everyone feels guilty that they didn't say more, do more, try harder to prevent a death.

Daniella Joseph finds it hard to celebrate her own birthday. At the end of her own ninth birthday celebrations, after a party in a local community centre in February 1988, her two-year-old sister Sharona was snatched and murdered. The terrible murder received maximum publicity at the time it occurred.

The circumstances were that Daniella was 'looking after' Sharona in the playground adjoining the centre while her parents cleared up inside. She let go of Sharona's hand for a split second to follow a friend. During that fateful second, a disturbed twelve-year-old boy who had been loitering in the playground abducted Sharona and murdered her. Daniella has tortured herself and blamed herself for her sister's death ever since.

'If I had looked after my sister, as my mother asked, she would still be here. But I let go of her hand to run after one of my friends. I left her alone,' she told Lesley Gibson in an interview in the *Daily Mail*. 'I blame myself and I hate myself as much as I hate her killer because I gave him the opportunity to murder her. I knew she was vulnerable. I had loved and protected her since the day she was born. I should have been protecting her when she needed me most but I let her down. I'm stuck in the moment when I let go of Sharona's hand and I can't move on.'

Of course, it could not be Daniella's fault. How could a nine-year-old be held accountable for the actions of one, deeply disturbed and sick teenager who was lurking, intent on his evil plan? She might just have easily bent down with her back turned to tie a shoelace as to listen to her friend.

Daniella has spent years undergoing psychotherapy and counselling to help her rid herself of these terrible feelings of guilt. Countless people, including her parents, have tried to persuade her that, as she was only a child herself when her sister was killed, she is in no way blameworthy. 'At one time, I became suicidal. The only thing that stopped me killing myself was my parents and my brother. I couldn't bear to put them through any more pain,' she said.

There are a number of specialist organisations offering counselling for children who have been bereaved, including CRUSE, the National Association of Bereavement Services, Parentline and Young Minds Parents Information Service.

Trauma

Children who have witnessed a traumatic death, such as a murder, been involved in a disastrous accident or crash, or who have lost their homes and loved ones in something such as a gas explosion or a war zone, may need specialised help and treatment in order to come to terms with their loss and be able to go forward from the tragedy.

If there has been a tragedy at school, such as the death of a classmate on a school trip, parents and schools may need expert help, too. Such experiences, says Dr Judd, 'are often too shocking and disruptive to be absorbed and worked through over time without expert guidance and help. What is important is helping children who have witnessed such an event to recover.'

The Children's Team at the Trauma Stress Clinic (73 Charlotte Street, London W1T 4PX – tel: 020 8530 3666) in London are experts in helping children, parents and teachers through death which has occurred in traumatic circumstances.

The Childhood Bereavement Project has been working since 1998 – as a multi-agency, national initiative – to ensure that all children can access the information, guidance and support they need to enable them to manage the impact of death on their lives. As a co-ordinating body, their role is to promote and co-ordinate collective action and work in partnership with service providers to both improve the range and quality of bereavement support for children throughout the UK and to increase access to information, guidance and support services. Contact them at Huntingdon House, 278–290 Huntingdon Street, Nottingham NG1 3LY, telephone them on 0115 911 8070 or visit their website: www.ncb.org.uk.

8

Friendship

'Friends and neighbours – though your house may be tumbling down
– if you've got friends and neighbours – you're the richest man in town!'
Billy Cotton and his band

When bereavement strikes at the heart of your family, friendships become an asset more valuable than any other you possess. Yet they may also be hard to retain on the old familiar basis once the shock of the moment recedes and is replaced by the illogical belief that the death has in some way 'tainted' the survivors and may, like chicken-pox, be 'catching'.

The fact is that when you are widowed, you are no longer part of the 'normal' family set-up. Where friends may have been happy to share their weekends and bank holidays with you when you were a 'whole' family, they may not be quite sure what to do with you when you are widowed, or when you have lost a child. They may feel awkward about having what you have lost. They may feel that they will hurt you if they invite you to share the activities you once shared as friends. They may feel embarrassed in case their family modus vivendi reminds you too sharply of what you once had. And, of course, if you're absolutely honest, there are times when hurt it will. Nevertheless, life does go on regardless of anyone's personal circumstances and unless you decide to become a hermit and exclude yourself from the world you have to make a choice about when to rejoin as an active member of the human race.

Peter White says that his friends were anxious to ensure he never left the cocoon of their care, throughout his wife Sandy's two-year illness, as well as after her death.

'We all knew what was ahead, including Sandy,' he says. 'She was in a hospice at the end. It was November and we all knew that it was getting fairly close. A friend took me aside and said that if anything happened before Christmas, he and his family would like my son and I to spend Christmas with them. I knew from when the invitation was issued that it wasn't being done out of duty or pity. They felt no obligation to invite us. The invitation was there and it was a great comfort when Sandy died later that month that the pressure of: "Oh God, how are we going to cope with Christmas?" had been removed.'

Not everyone who is bereaved has quite such caring friends or is quite so lucky. But, if you feel that old friends are staying away, and you miss them desperately, there are a number of ways in which you can encourage them to return. It may take a bit of courage on your part – but how much better it feels to be admired for what you can achieve rather than pitied for what you can't.

Here's a courage checklist, see how you score:

1. You have walked alone into a room full of strangers, possibly for the first time. Whether they were accountants, solicitors or other professionals with whom you needed to deal or whether they were acquaintances, you have done it – and you've survived.
2. You have dealt with living essentials (such as paying household bills, writing cheques, cooking a meal, doing the washing, organising child- or parent-care) and spoken with authority to people who matter in a way you never needed to before your bereavement.
3. You have been able to organise financial matters for yourself. This may have involved finding a new job, to fit in with your

changed home circumstances, in a field which may not have occurred to you in the past.

4. You have discovered the ability to tell people exactly how you feel and what you want.

5. You can make choices for yourself. This does take practice – and you will make mistakes – but at least you will know that the mistakes are your own.

What has all this to do with friendship? A great deal. *Because if you have found the courage to do only one or two of the above, then you have the courage to take the lead and tell your friends what you need from them.*

Weekends and bank holidays are by their very nature times when families and friends seize the opportunity to get out and about or join together for pleasure. They may be scared to ask you to join them. That's where your lead is essential. In most other circumstances, if you are hurting you expect other people to take you by the hand and lead you to safety. But death is frightening. Think back to when someone else you know lost a loved one. You didn't know what to say. You didn't know what to do. You didn't want to cause unnecessary pain to someone who was obviously in mental agony. Well, now that's YOU. If you don't tell people what you want, no one can second-guess you. So be brave enough to open your mouth. There's no law that says you can't pick up the phone, ask them what they are doing, e*xactly as you might have done before your bereavement*, and then when they tell you, ask if you can join them, if it's appropriate to do so. Spell out your needs if you have to. Say:

- I enjoy your family's company so much.
- It won't bother me to see you all together. In fact, it will give me great pleasure and remind me of the happy times we used to have as a family.
- I need to start living again and because you're such close friends, I feel I can ask you to help me by treating me as a whole person.

Peter White says that one of the invitations he will always remember with gratitude was one issued just two weeks after Sandy's death:

'My friends were having a dinner party and rang to invite me but asked if I thought it was "too soon" to go out. As a couple we had spent many happy evenings there and I didn't see why I shouldn't go this time. Of course, it felt strange walking into the room on my own. But what good would I have done staying at home? All I would have done was mope all evening.'

Of course, there are times when you will be in company and suddenly feel very jealous of the relationship of those around you. Anger you may have thought buried may surface with a vengeance. You may find yourself having to turn your back as tears well uninvited and unexpectedly at the 'normality' which everyone else seems to enjoy but which you are denied. You may think: 'Why should this have happened to me?' I think the only answer to that is: 'Why not?' It sounds somewhat morbid to say that the only thing that is certain when we are born is that we will all die, leaving loved ones mourning us, but it is true. Sadly, death is something that afflicts every one of us at some time in our lives, some earlier than others, some later. Parents, partners and sometimes children die. All of us need friends when someone close to us dies.

Angela, who lost her husband Tony eleven years ago, says: 'Many friends tell me that they lose their married friends after bereavement. I can understand why. Even all these years down the line, I find it quite hard to go to a dinner party and find myself the only single person there. The world is full of married people and when I hear them talking about motoring tours across France or weekends away or just dining out once a week, I find myself feeling uncomfortable and – if I'm honest – envious. These are the things Tony and I should have been doing now that our children are grown up. They are things I can't do alone, and no one thinks to invite me along as they might have suggested when I was half of a couple. So now I often refuse invitations to evenings where such things may crop up. I do tell people why. I don't think they understand and I'm sure they talk about me – but I don't care any more. I'm concerned to protect myself because if I don't, no one else will.'

Angela admits she is lonely and as time goes by, her pain is worsening. She also admits it is her own fault. Seeing others who have the relationship you wish you had can indeed be very painful. But far, far better to see them, and even to some degree share the warmth and human contact they engender, and ask to be included if no one thinks to ask you, than to be excluded entirely and sit home alone, simmering with jealousy and resentment. You are not the only person in the universe in this situation, no matter how lonely and isolated you feel. If you want to join the living world again, YOU have to do something about it.

Death ISN'T catching

When Laurie and her husband Roger's baby daughter Rebecca (sick from birth as the result of a genetic disorder which meant her brain couldn't develop properly) died at the age of ten months, she says the family which included Elizabeth, then aged three, became 'social pariahs'.

'Our friends were doubly shocked by our tragedy. There suddenly seemed to be a strong feeling that because we lived in a community where people had two children, we might be "bad news". It was as though they were thinking: "If this can happen to Laurie and Rog, then it can happen to us."'

Laurie and Roger say that although people were generally 'wonderful' initially, their reactions later left them feeling socially excluded. 'We became almost public property in our village. We were the family that had endured this "terrible tragedy", and they didn't let their children come to Becky's funeral, or later to the memorial service we held to give thanks for her life, because they thought it was wrong to expose them to death. Elizabeth was the only small person there, and we know that people thought we were wrong to include her. It wasn't for them to judge.

'Immediately after the funeral we received an awful lot of attention. But then the attention waned and Elizabeth and I were almost like social lepers. People weren't sure whether to invite us to things or not – as though we might in some way remind them of their own family's frailty or their own vulnerability.

'We held a memorial service for Rebecca, later. This was a service for her, but it was also a service to support the whole family and Elizabeth was, and is still, very much a part of that whole family which does and always will include Rebecca. But our loss set us apart.'

When friends hurt

Many women (and some men) who have lost their partners claim that after the initial support network falls away (usually between six months and a year after the death), the invitations dwindle. 'Friends', no longer casting themselves in the 'I can do good, here' role, feel they have done their duty and can do no more. They expect you to have 'got over it' and be 'back to normal'. Although men may immediately find themselves in great demand at a social occasion where other single women will be present, many women alone report they feel 'ignored', as though their lone status makes them easy prey for husbands with a wayward inclination.

'I had several friends who were very kind at the beginning,' says Anna. 'One couple in particular had both been bereaved themselves and were on a second marriage, so I was convinced I would find them supportive. However, their visits – and invitations – fell away. I admit some of it may have been my own fault. I accepted invitations but didn't repay them because I found it too much effort and too painful. I used to ring my friends frequently, but the calls were returned less and less often and in the end I decided I couldn't have a one-way friendship. I was particularly hurt because my late husband and I were particularly good to the husband when he was bereaved. He was married to one of my childhood friends. I am convinced his second wife saw me as a threat, although I had never given her any reason to do so. I don't hear from them any more and I don't want to – although I know that if we did meet up, they'd say: "We must get together some time." That's one phrase I've learned to hate.'

I have to say that I was lucky. My friends of thirteen years ago are, for the most part, my friends today. But there were exceptions. When I moved house, I determined never to ask any man to help me with a task I could pay to have done professionally – on the basis that I could not then be accused of 'finding an excuse' to be alone with another woman's husband. The fact that, at that stage, I could no more counter any man, even my closest friends' husbands, putting a friendly arm around my shoulder or pecking me on the cheek in public as they had always done, was not something I talked about.

On one occasion, I was entertaining some old friends on a filthy November night when all the electricity downstairs blew. I went into the kitchen to reset the fuse and one of my friends' husbands followed me. I told him that I knew what the problem was. I had recently moved into a brand new house and was waiting for the electrician to put the light fitting up outside the back door. The wires, although sealed, were averse to water, and every time it rained, the fuse box blew. He had recently been made redundant and was free during the daytime and he offered, in front of his wife and other guests, to 'save me the money' and to come and fit the light fitting I had bought, and which was sitting on a counter top, on the following Monday. I accepted gratefully.

He appeared as promised Monday morning, fitted my light, had a cup of coffee and left. Later that day, his wife called. 'Don't you *ever* ask my husband to help you again,' she said angrily. I was furious as the penny dropped. Unsure of her own relationship, she cast me in the 'other woman' role. I gave her a piece of my mind – and told her I wouldn't have her husband – or for that matter anyone else's husband – if they were presented to me tied up in ribbons. We still speak. I don't think her husband has a clue what his wife said, but the close relationship we had during my first husband's life has gone for ever.

The friends who mean the most

On the other side of the coin are the two couples who were acquaintances rather than friends before my husband's death. They became the closest friends anyone could wish for. They made it their business to make me feel that they invited me because they enjoyed my company. They gave me the sense that I was able to add something to *their* lives. When I was with them, I never felt like a 'deserving charity'. They constantly invited me to join them if I was at a loose end on Saturday evenings, bank holidays and even invited me to share weekends away. One of the wives even 'loaned' me her husband when I was selling my home, so that when strange people came to view carpets, curtains and other major items, it wouldn't look to the outside world that I was a 'woman alone'. For those friends, who have become as brothers and sisters, I will always be truly indebted.

Getting 'over' it

As the person who has been bereaved slowly accepts their new social situation, so others may feel it is time for the bereaved to 'pull themselves together' and 'get over it'. Of course, you never do 'get over' bereavement. As I've said before, you are never going to be quite the same person again as you were in the past. But, by accepting and returning invitations, you can persuade others to believe that you are 'back to yourself' again and find yourself in a totally accepting and acceptable social situation. Invitations you extend to others whose company you enjoy generally mean you will be invited again on a reciprocal basis. Friendships are give and take, no matter what your social status. Whether married, single, widowed, divorced or just landed from Mars, if you don't invite people to your home, then you can't expect a never-ending stream of invitations back again.

Few couples who have not known the experience of being alone can understand that bereavement does strip people of their self-confidence. Equally, it may feel a great burden to undertake entertaining when you have just lost a parent and especially hard if you have lost a child. But it's something you need to work at.

There are a whole variety of ways of 'coping' with friendships. I employed the following tactics. I decided that, socially, I would not be disadvantaged by 'the amputation' of my husband – and that the only way to go forward was to behave as I always had.

If you are bereaved and lonely:

- Accept only the invitations of old friends where you know you may feel comfortable. It is perfectly acceptable to ask who else will be at a social gathering or dinner party and if you don't feel like going, be honest and up-front and say so – but do emphasise that you love being invited and hope they will ask another time.
- Don't be embarrassed about your social status. If you decide to accept an invitation, and find yourself among strangers who may have no knowledge of your status (unless they've been pre-warned by your host/hostess), it is perfectly acceptable to say that you are bereaved before joining in the general conversation.
- Don't get drawn into explanations about what happened. Have the courage to close the subject by saying: 'I'd rather not discuss that now' and turning to something else.
- If you enjoy dining out or going out for a drink, let friends know that you would like to join them, just as you did when you were four rather than three. Insist that you will pay your way, just as you've done in the past. Although many men may find it demeaning or treading on their pride to take a woman's money, explain to their wives that you will be happy to split the bill three ways instead of in half as you used to – and that you will settle up afterwards so there can be no embarrassment at the table. There's no reason why men can't behave in precisely the same way and that way, you can enjoy a meal out in company you enjoy without feeling you are a 'burden'.
- If you are asked to a dinner party, return the invitation. It may not be easy to entertain alone – indeed, initially, it can be devastatingly difficult. You don't have to cook every morsel, thanks to the wonders of ready-prepared dishes and M & S. It needn't cost you a fortune. Pasta and salad is generally a welcome menu, followed by a ready-made desert if you're not up to creating one – although creating food to give pleasure to others, I discovered, can be quite therapeutic.

I won't pretend that entertaining alone is easy. The first few times I did it, I was fine during the preparation – because my husband was never around when I cooked anyway. The hard part was clearing up alone after everyone had gone. At the beginning, I made the mistake of refusing all offers of help and then landing up in floods of tears in a heap over the destructed remains of the meal because clearing up was a chore we'd always tackled together. From then on, I accepted help clearing the table – and I think my friends were happier knowing that they hadn't abandoned me in a mess.

Situations

Of course, behaving as you have always behaved can lead to some sticky (and totally innocent) situations. Like most bereaved people, it took a long time for me to realise that I couldn't issue invitations in the way I had always done without being suspected of ulterior motives.

I had once planned a family Sunday lunch, including my daughters, my sister-in-law and a couple of friends. I went out on a first date (a blind date) about eighteen months after my husband's death and we had a lovely evening. When the evening was over, he asked what I was doing the following day. I told him I was busy entertaining – and he looked somewhat sad and said he had nothing to do all day. So without thinking further, I said: 'Why don't you come too?' The perfect gentleman (and he too was a widower), he said he would have to give it some thought. 'You see,' he explained, 'If you introduce me to your family, I could take it to mean that you have other ideas up your sleeve for when they've left – and they could take it to mean that this was a serious relationship and we had something to tell them.' And all I had intended was to feed Sunday lunch to a lonely man – just as I might have done when I was married.

Take action – now!
- Draw up a list of all the people to whom you 'owe' invitations.
- Try, where possible, to mix marrieds and singles.
- Look for the easiest way *for you*. Many women particularly find it easier to entertain at lunchtime than in the evening. Barbecues

are brilliantly non-formal ways of returning invitations; or you might try for a bridge party or a Trivial Pursuits evening where everyone can join in and have fun.

- Ask one or two of the men to take over the 'drinks' routine. Men can entertain too and not being able to cook is no excuse. Invite everyone to 'bring a dish' and have a 'guess-who-made-it' party.

Be careful about who you invite, where you invite them and what to. Many women make the mistake of accepting a 'first date' (as I did) and then behaving entirely inappropriately in all innocence.

Pietro tells how he took out a lady whose telephone number he had been given:

'I collected her from her home and we had a lovely day,' he says, 'although it was quite clear from the start to me that she wasn't my sort of lady. I dropped her home and she said: "You must come in and have a cup of tea." It seemed churlish to refuse, so in I went and there was a tea trolley, beautifully laid with currant bread and jam and cakes. We'd just eaten a huge lunch but I politely waded my way through tea and said I had to go. "Oh," she said, "but I've made you supper." With that she led me into the front room where the table was laid for two – and she proceeded to extract a magnificent cold meal from the refrigerator. How could I refuse? It would have been rude. We sat down to eat and as I picked at my supper I realised why she was rather broad. She offered me wine, and when I declined because I was driving she insisted I could stay the night if I chose. At that point, I made a bolt for the door!'

How to be a treasured friend

So far, the talk about friends has been how someone who has been bereaved can cherish treasured friendships. But how can YOU be a real friend to someone who has already lost such a large chunk of their life. The first thing is BE THERE. Don't shy away for fear of saying or doing the wrong thing. As I said earlier, death isn't catching. Better to get it slightly wrong than to be one of those who crosses the road to avoid facing 'embarrassment'.

Please DON'T tell your friend that they will 'get over it' or that 'time heals'. Those are probably the two worst, and most untrue cliches in any book. Time does, of course, round off the rough edges of raw pain, but bereavement is an incision into the spirit of mourners and, like any cut, it will always leave a scar. You have to realise that the experience of death changes us all and your bereaved friend will never be quite the same again.

What do you say?

This is a tough one, even for those of us who have suffered a close bereavement ourselves. When you meet someone for the first time since their bereavement, what on earth can you *say* to them that will offer them comfort? The first thing is to acknowledge what's happened. It may mean just saying: 'I heard you lost – [your mother, father, sister, brother, husband, wife, child] – I'm truly sorry.' This breaks the horror barrier. If you knew the person who died, say something kind about them. It may just be: 'I'll never forget that lovely voice/smile/wit.' If you didn't know them, then turn the compliment round: 'Your parent must have been very special to have had a son/daughter like you.' Or: 'I know that our mutual friends always spoke so well of your partner.'

Once you've acknowledged their loss, be prepared for tears, especially if the bereavement is very new. They're normal – and it's fine for you to share in them. A touch, a stroke of a hand, a hug or simply a handshake, depending on how well you know the person who is grieving, can say more than any words.

- *Don't* tell someone who is obviously looking and feeling terrible how well or wonderful they look or how well they appear to be doing. If the death is recent, they're probably in limbo – so leave it alone.
- Ask after their children, or other relatives. Their loss hasn't set them aside from the rest of the human race. But, please don't ask for gory details, no matter how curious you may be to hear what *really* happened. If the bereaved person wants to tell you, they will. If they'd rather not, they probably won't. If you know what

happened, save them the anguish of wondering whether you know or not. You could say something like: 'Jerry told me what happened and I do feel for you.'

- Ask them if there is anything you can do – if you really think you can help. If you can't, or don't know them too well, don't make an offer. Don't look at them with sad eyes, and please don't use false tones of sadness. When you're feeling rock bottom, the last thing you want to feel is pitied – even if you, the helpless onlooker, pity them with all your heart.

Have you got staying power?

You may feel terribly sorry for someone who has suffered a death in the family and feel that it would be kind to keep in touch, even when you don't know them very well. *Don't offer more than you are prepared to give.* It's very easy to rush to the aid of someone in trouble, even a relative stranger. As a neighbour you may pop in and offer your help. If you offer, then be prepared to see it through. If you can't, then don't offer at all.

When people are feeling vulnerable after the death of a loved one, they will believe your offers and they may even take you up on them. If they find that your offer was only a lot of hot air, you may cause additional pain and distress for no good reason.

Making habits and breaking them

Here are some scenarios:

Your next door-neighbour's young wife dies. He has to go to work. He's worried about who is going to care for his children when they come home from school. He has to work and although his employers have been understanding, there is a limit to their compassionate leave. Grandparents live too far away to commit themselves on a daily basis and you have children at the same school. You have offered to 'help'. Do you:

- Offer to give the children tea every day and hang on to them until he comes home

- Suggest he gets a regular babysitter?

An acquaintance has lost a partner. Knowing you have been in a similar situation, a friend asks you to pop by and talk to her. Do you:

- Decline, saying you hardly know her so what's the point
- Write a note, saying that if they want to speak to you, they should give you a ring
- Write a letter or send a card of condolence and follow it up with a phone call and possibly a visit
- Pick up the phone and invite the other person round for a coffee or arrange to meet for a drink?

In these scenarios, the only answer is the one you feel capable of following through. Don't make promises you know you can't keep. If you know and like the children involved in the first scenario, then by all means agree to give it a 'try'. If you can't cope for any reason, it's up to you to be honest and say so. When you are bereaved and have been helped over the initial hurdles, it's very easy to fall into a false sense of feeling the world owes you a living. It is up to friends and acquaintances to make it clear, as tactfully as they can, that some things are not possible because they don't fit into your life style – and your life does go on as before.

Angus' son was fourteen and his daughter eleven when their mother died. 'I asked a neighbour for help and she agreed to have the children,' he says. 'One night, I was invited to a late meeting and asked her if she could hang on to them. She said she would but when I got home there was a babysitter in the house, minding all four children, because she'd had to go out. I was furious. She hadn't asked my permission to leave my children with a stranger.'

Their neighbour, Jill, described how she felt – she was justifiably furious. She had tried to help but she couldn't run her life around her neighbours' children, no matter how well-meaning she was. 'I had the children every day and he never even bought me a box of chocolates to say thank you,' she says. 'Then, when I had to go out and left my babysitter looking after his children at my expense, he had the cheek to complain. We don't talk any more.'

If only that neighbour had had the courage to be honest in the first place, and perhaps even ask for a small sum to cover 'tea' costs, she would not have felt so put-upon. It might not have ended in tears. Angus was the idiot for taking it for granted that once Jill had assumed some responsibilities for his children, she would take on those responsibilities at all times, regardless of her own situation.

Make sure that your generosity is not swayed by emotion into actions you will later regret. Think before you make offers or promises. Lay down the boundaries. Don't promise more than you can reasonably fulfil.

Keeping in touch

Do keep in touch with bereaved friends on a regular basis. However, this does NOT mean you have to ring them every single day, or even every week. Try to start out as you mean to go on.

Everyone rallies round a bereaved family during the first few months. It's amazing how cosseted this makes you (the bereaved) feel – and because they're *your* friends, you *know* they won't go away, except that some do!

One of my husband's business acquaintances rang me every single day for the first month – and I truly believed he and his wife cared about my family's welfare. He told me: 'No one misses your husband as much as I do.' It was a strange thing to say to a bereaved wife – but then people do say strange things.

The phone calls dropped to once a week, once a fortnight and finally just to high days and holy days. Finally, I was doing all the calling. My calls were never reciprocated. I did keep in touch (or tried to) with these people for many years. I felt hurt and terribly let down by their failure to reciprocate. I think they were among the 'you should be over it by now' brigade. As a real friend of someone who has been bereaved, it's worth knowing that nobody ever does get over bereavement, particularly if they've lost a young partner or a child. They may heal, but the scar will be part of them for ever.

I remember one of my late husband's dearest friends promised he wouldn't lose touch with me – but he did. At first, I rang him and his wife and tried to make arrangements to see them, but they were always 'so busy' and promised they would call me back – which they never did. I wish they'd been honest enough *not* to make promises they had no intention of keeping.

The husband did ring me once, on the first anniversary of my husband's death, just to 'remind' me that it was the first year! As if I could forget! After that, I never heard from him or his wife again. I met him in a shop about ten years later – he greeted me warmly as though we had only met the previous week, and asked me all the right questions about my girls. Then he began asking quite personal questions. I told him that if he'd bothered to keep in touch, he'd know the answers. He was obviously most put out by my reaction and probably by what he saw as my rudeness. But, as a result of my losses, I tend to be blunt and say exactly what I think, especially to people who offered unsolicited support and failed to deliver it.

Be aware:

Eating out, going to a film or the theatre or even for a long walk are really no fun alone. While singles holidays are growing in popularity, it is impossible for many single women to travel, even if they are self-confident enough to travel alone, for no better reason than that single supplements are generally prohibitively expensive.

If you know well someone who has been bereaved, do consider asking them to join you for a long weekend away on a strictly independent, self-paying basis – this can be a true act of friendship and mean more than you'll ever know.

Frances, widowed many years ago, says: 'I've been lucky because my friends allowed me to talk my heart out about Ben and then we all laughed together at the things he'd said and the times we had shared and that helped me through. Even when I was at my lowest and was lousy company, they kept on inviting me to things. Now I'm "normal" again, they accept me as I am, my own person.'

Angela has had a quite different experience. She says: 'Many people, particularly women, tell me that they lose their married friends after bereavement. I suppose it's my own fault that many of "our" friends have fallen by the wayside. I'm shy by nature and even eleven years down the line, I find it quite hard to go to a dinner party and find myself the only single person there.'

If you have a bereaved friend:

- DO listen when they need to talk – and if you find you can't, because you are busy, bored, or you feel you can't take it, say so kindly.
- DO go on inviting them over – possibly on an intimate, 'just you – we count you as one of our family' basis at first.
- DO ask *their* advice and discuss *your* problems with them – they haven't left the human race!
- DO keep it as simple and intimate as possible, particularly in the early days.
- DO talk about normal family incidents or regular annoyances in the presence of your bereaved friends without offering apologies. Nothing is more annoying than the kind of girly (or might it be manly) telephone conversation where your friend forgets and begins to complain about her husband's habit of littering the bedroom with his dirty socks – and then draws breath so hard you can literally see her hand cover her mouth as she says: 'I shouldn't be moaning to *you* about that.' My answer to that sort of comment has always been – 'Why not? Mine used to do exactly the same. I haven't forgotten what men are like.'
- DO be aware that there are many things from which single women in particular are excluded by virtue of their social status and which they may be missing.
- DO talk normally about the person who has died. Never fear to mention their name for fear of causing upset. 'Clearing' them out of a conversation is denying their existence.
- DON'T be offended if you invite a bereaved friend to join you and the invitation is subjected to the scrutiny of 'who else is on the guest list?', or if you are turned down. It may just be a bad day.

There may be a reason. Do give them a second (or third, or fourth) chance.

- DON'T be scared to invite a bereaved friend into 'mixed' company. Most men and women enjoy the normality of being in mixed company.
- DON'T make promises you have no intention of keeping.
- DON'T say to someone alone: 'Do keep in touch' or 'Do pop round'. They won't, because they will feel as if they're inviting themselves and that is uncomfortable.
- If you really mean that you'd love to see them – or even if you just feel you ought to – then *you* do the ringing, *you* issue a specific invitation, stipulating whether it's for a drink, a cup of tea, a meal, or whether there will be other guests.

The message is that your bereaved friends haven't stopped being your friends on account of their bereavement. Nor have they been disabled by the loss of their loved ones. They need your help to learn how to become whole people again in their own right and in order to do that, they need *your* support. Let them lead you where they want to go. Follow if you can. Take the lead yourself by suggesting positive means of support if you are able. By extending your friendship unreservedly in their times of trouble, you can be sure than when *you* need the hand of friendship, *they* will be there.

9

Sex and relationships

Up until now, I have tried to touch upon all kinds of bereavements, not only the death of a partner. This chapter, however, is aimed specifically at those who have lost their partners. Although I can only write personally from a widow's viewpoint, I believe that the same basics apply to anyone, male or female, whether they were living together, married, or in homosexual relationships, regardless of age or social status.

After the death of a beloved partner, nature is kind enough to numb us in many ways. Author, agony aunt and Relate-trained counsellor (Relate is the British Marriage Guidance Council) Suzie Hayman says, many men and women return from a funeral and the one thing they want and need above all others is the comfort of the missing person and to have sex with them.

'This is a recognised phenomenon after death,' says Suzie. 'People want sex as a way of reasserting their own survival and proof that they are still alive. Such feelings can be particularly confusing and upsetting when a much loved partner has died. They feel guilty and confused by this need.'

When you are first bereaved of a partner, I believe that, initially, you continue to survive on the love you once shared with your partner. It takes a long time before reality dawns and you realise that your partner is not able to reciprocate your physical love for them from beyond the grave. You will probably go on loving that person who shared more than their physical life with you for the rest of your life, no matter what future relationships you form. None will ever take the place of what you once had with a unique partner, and although subsequent partnerships may be wonderful, close and loving, they will never replicate what you had before because no two human beings are the same. Nor should you attempt to replicate a relationship. As a close friend who remarried very happily once told me: 'Comparisons are odious.' This is another person in a unique relationship with its very own characteristics.

It's obviously impossible to generalise, but in my limited experience, it would appear that women need longer to accept the death of their partner before embarking on a committed relationship. Men tend to fall into one of two distinct categories: those who cannot bear to be alone and commit themselves to subsequent relationships before their partners are 'cold in their graves', often to the consternation of those around them, and those who swear they will never look at another woman again, and who build shrines to their lost partner.

Denise Knowles, a senior counsellor and sex therapist with Relate, says: 'Many "shrine-builders" eventually do meet other partners with whom to share their lives and these partners may find themselves in the "Rebecca syndrome", sharing their lives with the ghost of their husband's dead partner.'

Suzie Hayman says: 'The difference in the way men and women react to the death of their partners can be put down to the fact the men may be far more mechanistic than women. There is an old joke that women will say: 'I love you' and men will demonstrate it. Women are verbal. They are looking for someone to express the emotions of love. Men are looking for someone to do it with. But at the end of the day, that doesn't mean that either gender is getting anything different.

Masturbation

For most people, love for a partner is fundamental to a normal healthy life. The emotion you share with a partner is the deepest emotion of all. Even those who no longer engage in full intercourse because of age or infirmity may have found enormous comfort in cuddling, kissing, hugging and touching because 'making love' has a far deeper meaning than the act of penetrative sex.

Sex is good for you. Doctors have proved scientifically that people in a stable sexual relationship are healthier and tend to live longer than those who are celibate. Satiating a healthy sexual appetite can be as vital to health as an appetite for food. When you are starved of sex as a result of death, the most normal thing to do is seek a way of satisfying that hunger in another way. You may not be able to maintain a balanced sexual 'diet' but most people do discover that there are more ways than one to crack a nut. This does not mean you need to rush out and sleep around.

All of us masturbate at some time in our lives. There is nothing dirty or sleazy about masturbation. It is nothing more than stimulating your own genitals to give pleasure. The smallest children do it because it feels good. Real sexual masturbation begins at puberty and it is a simple, totally safe way of finding sexual and emotional release.

Many people, particularly those who are middle-aged and older, may have been taught that 'playing with yourself', reading erotic books or using sex toys is not nice, naughty or even shameful. This is not true. Many people masturbate themselves and their partners as part of their normal, sexual relationship, both to pleasure themselves, pleasure their partners or show their partners what pleases them most. Sex therapists often recommend that people should masturbate in order to discover what pleases them most and share that knowledge with their partners so that they can fulfil one another's deepest needs.

When you are alone and bereaved, masturbation may not be the most fulfilling way of satisfying sexual hunger – but it may at least offer some temporary relief and comfort in a dire situation and, says

Suzie Hayman, it will not only give relief but bring pleasure.

'It is extremely important for people to recognise the pleasure in masturbation not just as a method of relief of loneliness or tension but as something that simply feels good,' she says. 'The myth is that if you masturbate, you are either lonely, sad or immature and that is just not true. Extremely mature, happily married couples masturbate. Masturbation is a way of giving yourself joy, so why not do it.'

And fantasy plays an important role here. Don't just masturbate 'under doctor's orders'. Enjoy wonderful fantasies. Imagine yourself kidnapped by your handsome gypsy lover or indeed back in your partner's arms. Use it as a way to celebrate the marriage you and your partner had. More importantly, use it to celebrate being a person who is able to move on as well as look back.

Elise allowed masturbation to work towards helping her release all her pent-up emotions after the death of her husband, Angus. She was forty-four when Angus died. She says: 'When you lose someone you love passionately, your whole life is in turmoil. Angus and I had a very passionate relationship. We laughed passionately. We rowed passionately. We loved passionately. When he died very suddenly, I didn't know what I wanted. I needed relief but I didn't know what kind of relief or where to get it. I think when you feel like that you overdose on everything.

'Some people overdose on chocolates, or tobacco or drink. I overdosed on masturbation. I think I must have masturbated more in the first two months after Angus' death than I had ever done before in my entire life. There was nothing wrong with it. I've talked to a lot of other bereaved people who say they found it helpful and I had no idea what else to do.'

Felice says: 'I didn't do anything for years. The thought of sex with anyone else was stomach churning. It was a good two years – and then I met somebody who was married, and I had an affair. When it ended, I missed the sex. At the time, I was reading a book with some fairly erotic chapters and one night, alone in bed, I found I was playing with myself as I read, almost without thinking. For the first time I brought myself to a climax. I felt tremendous release, relief and joy. After that I bought a 'top shelf' magazine and sent away for some sex toys. I began to enjoy what I was doing. I found I could give myself enormous comfort and pleasure by masturbating and what can be wrong about that?'

Are you ready for a relationship?

While you are still learning to accept the death of someone you've loved, it may seem impossible to contemplate ever accepting another partner to share your life with. You're never going to have another relationship, let alone sex, or are you?

The prospect that you may never know the closeness of another relationship may seem unbearably daunting, especially if you have been bereaved at a relatively young age. Yet you may suffer incredible pangs of guilt and feelings of disloyalty at the very thought of becoming involved in another close and loving relationship. In theory, you are single; in practice, your mind is still married. Until you can permit yourself to believe that you are not married any longer, you will not be ready to embark on dating.

Most couples do discuss 'What would happen if . . . ?' When the possibility that you might ever find yourself in such a situation seems remote, it is easy to say: 'Of course I wouldn't want you to spend the rest of your life alone. Of course I'd want you to be happy.' But when it comes down to the reality, the survivor may well ask themselves: 'I know what my partner said at the time, but were they telling the truth?'

Ask yourself the following:

- Do I enjoy my own company?
- Do I enjoy having my own space?
- Would my late partner really want me to spend the rest of my life alone? Think about what you would have wanted for them if the position had been reversed.
- Am I really ready for another relationship of any kind? If so,

what sort of relationship would I like? Companionship – someone with whom to share theatre or cinema outings and meals with no strings attached? A sexual relationship? A long-term relationship?

- If I did meet someone else, what sort of person am I looking for? What characteristics do I value – and what *don't* I want?
- Do I enjoy freedom from the chores occasioned by relationships – i.e. cooking, washing, ironing, sharing my TV, my music – perhaps my home?

If you can honestly answer 'yes' to the first two, then perhaps you are not ready – or maybe never will be – to share your life full-time again and it would be better to find a companion. Some couples are bogged down by excessive possessiveness in marriage, but most who have shared a full and loving relationship, free from anything other than 'normal' jealousy, can be sure that their partners would want them to find pleasure and enjoyment in their lives again.

Decide what you want to do with the rest of your life, and make plans as a single person – but be flexible enough to know that if you meet the right person you might be willing to change your plans. Be aware that if you go out actively seeking another partner, you may fall short of your own expectations. Go out looking for friendship rather than a relationship. Second relationships need time to grow and blossom just as first loves did and possibly more so. People rarely fall head-over-heels in love at first sight second time around. The chemistry of second relationships is different and often tempered by maturity.

Suzie Hayman says: 'One of the big problems of dating again is that people who have been in a relationship have forgotten the dating moves.'

- Learn how to flirt again. This may involve you in investing in a few 'young' magazines and 'borrowing' ideas.
- DON'T expect a new date to know the 'shorthand' you built up during a relationship which may have lasted ten or twenty years. It may come as quite a shock to realise someone you are going

out with doesn't know the 'in' jokes you and your previous partner shared.

- Accept that any relationships subsequent to bereavement will be new. In a new relationship, you need new, fresh 'touch-stones'.
- Accept that a new relationship, whether it be short- or long-term, will have value.
- Admit to yourself that if this is destined to be a short-term relationship, it can be 'played' at a less serious level. Don't expect too much. Having sex is fine if that's what you both want, without investing in enormous emotions.

Don't do anything or make any major decisions in a hurry. Certainly, during the first two years after I was bereaved, I didn't know what I wanted. One minute, I wanted to be alone for the rest of my life. The next, I craved marriage. I wanted to meet men – but the only man I wanted was my husband. I tortured myself because I couldn't make up my mind. I only found happiness again when I gave up teasing myself with what I couldn't have, accepted what I could, and gave up trying to change the unchangeable!

Almost without exception, both men and women who have had happy marriages (and some who have not) would love to find love in their lives again. However, achieving the right relationship may be more complicated than you imagine. If you set out on a mission to find love, you could find yourself jumping through fire-rimmed hoops.

The WAY Foundation (the initials stand for 'Widowed and Young') provides a self-help social and support network for men and women widowed under the age of fifty, and their children. The main aim is to help those widowed young to rebuild their lives by helping one another. Write to them at PO Box 74, Penarth, Cardiff CF64 5ZT, telephone them on 029 2071 1209 or visit their website: www.wayfoundation.org.uk.

How can I meet a new partner?

Introductions

Friends may well introduce you to someone they think may be 'suitable'. Ask them to tell you if they're planning any such encounters because it's far easier if you are forewarned. If you don't like the person to whom you have been introduced, it may be as well to inform your well-meaning host or hostess that they're 'very nice, but not for me'. But do give the other person a chance and sometimes a date on a one-to-one basis will offer a fairer impression than the awkwardness of being 'in company'.

Shared interests

You may well meet someone as you 'carry on' with your life. Join activity clubs such as bridge, swimming or a gym – or perhaps evening school for the sheer pleasure of doing something or learning something you may never have had the opportunity to do or learn before. DON'T go along with the idea that you are going out to find a mate. If you do meet someone interesting, consider it a bonus.

Dating agencies

Check that the agency you sign with will actually be able to offer you suitable partners before you part with large sums of cash. Some women over the age of forty may be horrified to discover they are often considered 'too old' to be taken on to an agency's books!

Newspapers and the Internet

Many happy relationships begin this way – but do take some simple safety precautions if you have agreed to meet a stranger through a newspaper ad or an Internet encounter. Women in particular should ensure they:

- Arrange to meet in a public place.
- Take a land-line phone number (not a mobile number) so that you can ring them back and check the person you are meeting is

who and where they say they are. Women should *only* give their mobile phone numbers to strangers.

- Tell someone else who you are meeting and where and give a rough idea of what time you should be home. Give your friend the land-line phone number of the man you are meeting.
- If you are meeting a stranger for the first time, why not suggest a foursome so that you have the safety net of friends who can rescue you in an awkward situation.
- You might suggest to a couple of friends that they have a drink in the bar where you are meeting so that should it turn unpleasant, or you feel in any way compromised, you can make an excuse and join them. Trust your instincts. If the other person makes you feel at all uneasy, bail out.

Look through the Lonely Hearts ads – but be warned. You need to learn the hidden lingo. Try this as a dictionary:

Men advertise:
- Intelligent – is happy to discuss cars as well as booze and his former birds.
- GSOH – has a stock of jokes and you need to be prepared to listen to repetitions each time he meets another set of your friends.
- Medical consultant – not necessarily a doctor (he didn't say he *was*!) Could be male nurse, chiropodist, chiropractor – or just enjoy being consulted about your menopause.
- Educated – can read.
- Outgoing – loves being the centre of attention.
- Likes animals – shares his home with an Alsatian which must go on all dates.
- Loving – octopus on first date.
- Sporty – likes watching the Grand Prix on TV.
- Slightly paunchy – has a beer belly.
- Semi-retired – layabout.
- Practically baggage free – loves talking about the baggage he does have whenever the chance arises.
- N/S – probably violently anti-cigarettes.

Women advertise:

- GSOH – laughs at every joke he tells, no matter how many times she's heard it before.
- Sporty – goes to the gym five times a week. Likely to be on a diet. Gourmets beware.
- Elegant – spends a fortune on clothes.
- Petite – five feet tall – possibly five feet wide.
- Cuddly – fat.
- Vivacious – loud.
- Bubbly – loud.
- N/S – and don't bring a cigar near her, either.

This may be tongue-in-cheek, but as Denise Knowles says: 'It is important to recognise when you are ready to think about dating.' She suggests you ask yourself a number of questions:

- If I do this, how am I going to feel?
- Is there something holding me back? What?
- Am I feeling guilty – perhaps because I still 'feel married'?
- Would dating make me disloyal to my late partner?
- Would my late partner think the person I am dating is suitable for me?
- What will other people say?

Once again, the 'other people' are not living your life and have no right to be judgemental. If you feel ready to go for another relationship, the only way to start is with a first date – and you need to give yourself permission to be free. That is the only way you will ever be able to move forward.

Singles clubs may not be your scene, but they do offer the advantage of meeting face-to-face. Most people can sum up another human being within twenty seconds of first setting eyes on them. Try to find a club for widows and widowers – they do exist. If there is no such club in your area, why not start one, either by placing an advert in your local newspaper or putting a request for other people in the same situation to get in touch with you through your church, synagogue, temple or mosque newsletter. You may be amazed at the number of people who get in touch and who have been looking for exactly the same things as you are. You may not meet a mate, but you will gather around yourself single friends of both sexes. Nothing is as important as having a good and reliable same-sex 'best' friend.

If you find yourself somewhere you don't want to be, don't despair. It really is very difficult – and I think you have to be incredibly brave – to hit the so-called 'singles scene' again. The trouble is that many of those who do attend singles functions forget they are middle-aged and behave as though they are eighteen again. You may end up feeling totally out of place. Remember, you don't *have* to go again. In fact you don't *have* to do anything you don't want to do, ever.

Dating

In his latest book *Why Can't I Fall in Love?*, self-styled love guru Shmuley Boteach says that before you fall in love, it is necessary to 'fall in like' with someone. That is certainly a sentiment I echo. He suggests that anyone looking for love should behave like a 'mental virgin'. In other words, he suggests that too much sex with no meaning attached to it can cause such a jaded attitude that sex becomes a bore and that it is perfectly legitimate to opt out of having sex for sex's sake.

Even if you have been married or in a long-term relationship in the past, no one has the right to take away your innocence and your right to say: 'Thanks, but no thanks.' It doesn't make you a prude.

'Experience has given us too much knowledge; it's violated our private spaces and left our emotional nerve endings raw and exposed. We've all lost our virginity emotionally,' he says. 'We feel frustrated and in despair because we fear we can never recover it. The truth is that we can.'

I have been looking for a joke book, dealing solely with the antics of middle-aged dating, that could match the experiences that I and some of my widowed and widowered friends have encountered. As

I haven't been able to find one, perhaps I'll be tempted to write one myself at some time in the future. Ask anyone over the age of thirty-five who has lost a partner – whether through death or the death of a previous relationship such as divorce – to talk of their dating experiences and I guarantee that you will 'rofl' – computer talk for 'roll on the floor laughing'.

The most obvious of all ways to meet is introductions by friends – or friends of friends. There are always relatives, friends and acquaintances who want to see you 'paired'. Sometimes, and with the best of intentions, almost before your beloved partner has been buried! One acquaintance rang me about two months after my husband had died, and at a time when meeting and mating was possibly the last thing on my mind. She said she had some 'sad' news for me.

'There was this lovely widowed man I thought I'd introduce you to in a few months' time when you were ready,' she told me, 'but you'll never believe it. He dropped dead this morning.'

Pietro recalls some of his dating experiences with amusement. 'I set up a blind date, after responding to an advertisement in the local paper, with a lady who sounded absolutely delightful on the phone,' he smiles. 'We chatted for ages and appeared to have a lot in common. She told me she was forty-six, had a twenty-year-old daughter and an eighteen-year-old son. We arranged to meet in a restaurant for lunch.'

When he arrived, Pietro says, he looked around for the small, dark-haired lady of her description. 'I saw this very short, very fat lady standing at the entrance, clearly looking to meet someone and to my horror, I realised she was my date,' he says. 'We introduced ourselves and I saw that she looked nearer sixty than forty-six.'

Dating rules:

Shmuley Boteach advises that if you meet a new date and don't dislike what you see but don't instantly feel an attraction, it is still important to give the relationship time to work. 'First appearances can be deceptive and someone who is not instantly attractive on the outside may be deeply attractive from within,' he says. 'Men are the worst culprits when it comes to instant appeal. If they meet a woman who doesn't have an hour-glass figure, beautiful hair, lovely skin they may dismiss her as unsuitable before she has said a word. Yet, it may take time for common factors to become visible and to discover what is behind the façade, and they may well miss out on the chance of a partner for no better reason than time.'

When you meet someone for the first time:

- Discover what you have in common.
- Discover where you disagree.
- If you are not instantly attracted, give the relationship a chance.
- If it is clearly not for you, then say so.
- Don't date just anyone for the sake of assuaging loneliness. It's better to be alone than with someone you can't stand.
- Above ALL, trust your *own* judgement: you know yourself better than anyone else in the world.

Flings

Many of us indulge in 'flings' after the death of someone we love, as did Marisa.

'He was very charming, quite persuasive and totally unsuitable as a future partner,' she says. 'In my saner moments, I wouldn't have given him another glance. Having been a virgin when I married first time around, and monogamous thereafter, I was also fairly ignorant. He bought me a present. The *Joy of Love*, the definitive sex manual by Alex Comfort.

'At any other time, I might have taken such a "gift" as an insult, but I was fascinated by it. I wanted to try everything in it. Immediately. And then, when the fling was over, I was deeply ashamed of myself for having behaved in such a totally reckless (to my lifestyle and upbringing) way. When I told my bereavement counsellor during the course of one of our sessions, she said: "There's nothing to be ashamed of. You weren't being promiscuous. It was what you needed at that time." '

However, Marisa admits that, on one score, she did behave irresponsibly. 'I think probably I was being rather more stupid than my bereavement counsellor suggested,' she says. 'With so much emotion, so much adrenaline, so many confused hormones rushing round my body at the rate of a high-speed train, and post-hysterectomy with the dangers of pregnancy removed, I didn't stop to think of sexually transmitted diseases or AIDS. I did ask him to wear a condom. When he declined, I sort of thought it would be all right. I knew people he knew, didn't I? How that could have offered me protection, I don't know. He was clearly highly sexed and as someone has since reaffirmed to me, an erect penis knows no morals. If this man, quite clearly experienced in love-making, was so ready to jump into bed with me, he had probably done it a hundred times before with a hundred other women and who knows who else his former partners had gone to bed with!'

She is not the only idiot on the block . . .

Elise says: 'After Angus' death, I made myself a fantasy list of all the things I wanted to do, the sort of things I never would have dreamed of doing during his lifetime. One of the things on my list was to have a madly passionate fling. I did it and I enjoyed it. I wasn't in the least ashamed of doing it. It was just something else to tick off my list and get out of my system.'

Gabrielle says that after her husband died, the thought of being with another man turned her stomach – but, she admits, the thought of being on her own was even more scary.

'Two years after my husband's death, I met a married man at the swimming pool. I saw him there virtually every day. I wasn't immediately attracted to him but we became friends. It never occurred to me to have sex with him until we were in a bookshop and I felt his breath on my neck. It sounds novelesque but it was true.

'About two weeks after that, we went out together, he came back to my place and we went to bed. I felt very guilty about it on more than one count. I felt guilty because I felt I was betraying my husband. I felt awful because he was married. But the sex was amazing. It was as though I had been woken up. As though someone switched me on again. I wanted more and more. We used to get up to all sorts of games, in a shared changing room and at home. Wherever the possibility presented itself. We used to go to bed three or four times a week.

'It went on for five years. I always knew that it could never be anything more than an affair. It ended because it had run its course. We are still friends. He would like to start it again but I've said there's no point.

'I've had a couple of sexual encounters since then. It's not just sex I want. It's a loving relationship. I want the fireworks and the music as well. As yet, it hasn't happened. I think when you've had one good, solid, loving and sexually fulfilling relationship you always want more.'

Mating

Apart from giving yourself permission, the only other people whose approval you need are your children. Denise Knowles suggests that if you are planning to date regularly with one single person, it is important to draw your children into the equation.

'If it looks as though this situation is going somewhere, get your children to meet your date,' she says. 'When you introduce them, don't do it by presenting your date as a parental replacement but just as "someone who can make me happy again and someone with whom I would like to spend some time".' Parents need to acknowledge that children have been bereaved and are suffering an irreplaceable loss, too.

'It is quite normal for children to go "Uugh" at the thought of their parents having sex and if you overlay that with their grief, the idea of you having sex with someone else can well colour their reactions both to you and your partner,' she says. 'Make it clear that neither of you are trying to take anyone else's place.'

Suzie Hayman points out, however, that your need for a relationship with a partner of your choice should not be dictated entirely by your children's views. 'You don't need your children's permission to date,' she says. 'You have the right to balance and negotiate with them if it looks as though the relationship is going somewhere. If they are very young, it may mean you take time, because there will come a time when they may leave home regardless of your situation. You need to look after yourself.'

Prenuptial agreements

So you decide to set up home together. Maybe to marry. If you are lucky enough to get a second 'bite of the cherry' of life, as I have been, it is plain common sense to set out in advance of the ceremony what belongs to whom and exactly what you are taking responsibility for, especially if one, or both, of you has children. You can do this by signing a prenuptial agreement.

Mike McCurley, a partner in McCurley Kinser McCurley & Nelson, Texan Matrimonial Lawyers, and President of the American Academy of Matrimonial Lawyers explains: 'It is all a matter of prioritising the obligations you incurred prior to meeting and marrying your next partner. When you are twenty and start a partnership in life, you take on obligations together, building your home with fairness, equality and parity. When you marry for a second time, one or both may have prior existing obligations and you need to be fair to those people as well as to one another.'

McCurley cites the case of Marilyn and Dwight Swanson of Beltsville, Maryland who were aged sixty-six and seventy-four respectively when they married five years ago, after meeting in a class called 'Dating After 50' at the local Holiday Park Senior Center.

Both were widowed, she after thirty-six years of marriage and he after almost fifty. She had one child and he had four. Mr Swanson has net assets of between two hundred thousand and three hundred thousand dollars as well as an annuity from his years as a meteorologist, climatologist and computer developer for the federal government. She has a pension for her first husband's work, and a social security cheque. 'I've seen examples where couples didn't have prenuptial agreements and the children were left with nothing,' says Mr Swanson. 'It was grossly unfair.'

He sold his house, earmarking most of the proceeds for his children, and moved into her bigger one. They counted up all their bank accounts and stocks and shares as well as household possessions, down to his TV and VCR. Now they keep track of everything they have bought since their marriage, from furniture to a patio they added to the house – and they note how much each has paid. If she dies, he can live in her house for five years before it goes to her child.

The law on prenuptial agreements varies from state to state in the US. But providing they are not drawn up under duress and meet other requirements, they are becoming law-enforceable throughout the country. In England, they have a moral rather than a legal standing, even if drawn up by lawyers.

However, the rewards of drawing up such agreements can go beyond legal security. Mary Cadet, a motivational speaker who leads the 'Dating After 50' workshops, where the Swansons met, says: 'It gets you in touch with your beliefs and values.'

10

Psychic help

'What is this death but a negligible accident?' asks Henry Scott Holland in his poem 'All is Well'.

When someone you care about dies, and no matter what the cause of death, whether sudden or expected, a release from pain and sickness or a tragic accident, suicide or murder, there are questions we all want answered to offer salve to our raw grief. Where have our loved ones gone? We may know what happened to their physical bodies, of course, but what about their souls, the individuality that made them who they were? Did it hurt to die? We can't see them, although we may dream about them constantly and be aware of their presence, but can they see us? Do they know what we're doing? Can they influence our fate? If religion cannot offer the answer we're seeking, can psychics help?

I remember falling asleep one afternoon the week after my own father died, and dreaming so vividly that he was there with me. I could feel his fingers gently stroking my cheek, just as he had done when I was a little girl. There was something he was trying to tell me, but just as he started to speak, the doorbell rang and woke me. Although that was sixteen years ago now, I remember cursing out loud because that contact for which I had yearned and which seemed to be within my grasp, had been so rudely snatched away.

I never did discover what it was he wanted to say and I have never been able to 'will' myself back into such a vivid dream about him since, although I've tried to coerce myself into such a dream-like state many times. To this day, I would still dearly love to be able to get in touch with my lovely dad and to know that he, like everyone else I have loved and who has died, is happy, peaceful and comfortable. As I write this, I can hear his old joke to the question: 'Are you comfortable, Dad?' 'No,' he would smile, raising one eyebrow in a special secret signal between us, 'But I make a living.' This need to hear him and others is not a morbid emotion but a need and a sensation common to everyone who has ever endured the pain of bereavement.

Inexplicable things do happen. Many sane and sensible people tell stories of how they 'felt' a presence or how 'coincidences' occurred following the death of someone they loved. There are, of course, always logical explanations. On one occasion, after my husband and my husband's brother-in-law had both died, I was sitting in the kitchen with my sister-in-law and the pair of us were reminiscing about how we both enjoyed (and missed) our morning cups of tea. All of a sudden, we heard the hiss and hum of the electric kettle that had apparently turned itself on. 'Just a short,' said an electrically-minded friend when I told him about it later. A coincidence! Was it? I don't suppose I'll ever know, but both of us, two reasonably intelligent and somewhat sceptical women, were freaked out to some degree by that electrical 'short'.

Common sense now tells me that believing the kettle switched itself on because of anything other than an electrical fault, is illogical. However, the idea that the two brothers-in-law, so close in life, might be sitting 'up there' on their little cloud, somewhere beyond our sight, looking down and having a chuckle between themselves about us was appealing. To think they might be able to hear and interpret our chat brought both of us comfort, despite the fact that both of us were totally committed to non-belief in an afterlife.

The bottom line is that the one thing we all pray for, whether or not we believe in life after death, is a 'sign' which will disprove our disbelieving selves and will show us that there is something of the person we have loved still here, and with us.

Science says that when brains no longer function, life as we know it has ceased. As the brain is the instrument of both emotion and memory, reasoning says that if the brain is dead, then all that it held in what Detective Hercule Poirot calls 'those little grey cells' must, necessarily, be gone too.

However, I have an open mind and, as with any other facet in the complicated questions surrounding death, this is no area for judgement. If seeking to contact a dead relative or friend through a psychic or medium will bring you some comfort or some peace of mind, then do it. Don't listen to people who give you all the reasons why you should not. They are not seeking what you are seeking – and once again the choice must be yours and yours alone. Forget what others will say or think about what you are doing. What matters most is finding consolation for a broken heart, and if that broken heart happens to be yours and you find a way to help soothe the pain, then go ahead.

Both the recognised clairvoyant mediums to whom I spoke while researching this book suggested a number of guidelines which may help you if this is a route you decide to follow:

- Go to someone who has been recommended to you, rather than making a spur-of-the-moment decision to have a casual reading at a psychic fair or on a seaside pier.
- Be prepared that the person you are most desperate to speak to may not 'come through' to order.

At the time you make your appointment do:

- *Check* what methods your chosen psychic plans to use – i.e. tarot card readings, dousing, aura reading, astrol psychometry or clairvoyance.
- *Ask* what will happen during the appointment, so you are aware of what to expect.

- *Don't* go to see anyone who asks personal questions at the time you make the appointment.
- *Don't* go with great expectations which will leave you disappointed and possibly in despair if you cannot reach the one you long to contact or if you discover that the person you are consulting actually comes up with nothing relevant.
- *Don't* be fooled into revealing too much of yourself, or your dead loved ones at the beginning of the meeting. The less you say, the better.
- *Don't* read too much into a generalised statement.
- *Don't* be too spooked if the person you are consulting comes out with amazing facts they could never have possibly known without 'help' from another place.

I cannot speak from personal experience on this one because I have never contacted a medium professionally, except during the course of writing this book, and even though the temptation was there then to 'get in touch' with all the members of my family who have died, I decided not to do it.

At various times in my life, most particularly immediately following my first husband's death, I felt an urgent and desperate need to somehow speak to him, to conclude the circle of our shared life and to be reassured that he was OK and at peace in a 'safe place'.

I was desperate to know that he would never leave us emotionally (and now I know he never will) and that he would somehow help us through the hardest part of losing his physical presence. I used to talk to him, at home, on trains, in the office. I used to stand by his grave (and sometimes still do, particularly when something happens which is a major part of what ought to have been our lives together – such as the marriage of our daughters and the birth of our grandchildren). Could a clairvoyant have helped me 'contact' him in a better way? I don't know.

The clairvoyants

There are some very experienced and clever mediums out there. Their 'gift' comes not only from spirit, but from the spirit within themselves which offers gentle coaxing and cajoling to bring relief to a suffering human soul. Make no mistake about it. Clairvoyants are counsellors, but of another kind and wearing a different hat. Some, like Lee Van Zahl, have formal counselling training as well as 'the gift'. Others, like Sally Morgan, have years of experience at bringing help at a time when it is needed most, and have a natural talent for offering consolation. If you believe you will find some solace from visiting a medium or clairvoyant, choose with care. As Sally Morgan says sensibly: 'Treat your choice of psychic as you would choose a dentist. Question other people who have been to see someone about how personal their knowledge was. What about their 'chair-side' manner. You must be comfortable with the person you are seeing.

Sally Morgan

Sally says she has known she had 'the gift' from as far back as she can remember. Even as a child, people would visit her home because, she says, without even realising what she was doing, she was able to 'see' people who weren't there physically and pass on messages, acting – she says, as an 'aerial' to relay messages from the 'other world'.

Sally, who writes newspaper and magazine columns about her 'contacts' with the dead and famous, is a jolly, round-faced, down-to-earth person who won't use tarot cards or crystals. At times, her talents have been employed by the police to help unearth gruesome criminal secrets. 'They only come to me as a last resort,' she jokes.

Her home is a suburban semi where baby grandchildren coo and gurgle merrily in the kitchen/family room, watched over by husband John as she counsels clients in her spotless little office at the front of the house. She is quick to affirm that she is most certainly *not* New Age. 'Counselling the bereaved is,' she says, 'an enormous responsibility.' She counsels hundreds, if not thousands, of bereaved people through her work as a clairvoyant and psychic every year, although she has no formal training.

She has two self-set golden rules:

- She will never tell anyone if she 'sees' that they or someone close to them is about to die.
- She will never counsel anyone under the age of twenty-one.

'Bereavement is a journey and it is a journey that I consider to be very well trodden. It is a path we all have to take some time. I think that the grieving in bereavement is a safety valve for our minds. When people come to me and say how confused, how isolated and how lonely they are, even when they are surrounded by their very close family and friends, they are wanting answers to what has happened. They may know exactly what caused the death, but even when someone is very old, it is someone they loved and they may want to know why it happened that way. Why did he or she have to leave me? Why did he or she die of pneumonia, or as a result of an accident? They cannot understand how their loved one could have been with them in body and spirit one moment and be gone the next. They don't necessarily want me to contact the person for them. What they really want is reassurance that if there is a place where our souls go after death, and, for want of a better word, we'll call it heaven because it has such a lovely sound to it, then that is where *their* loved ones are.

'When it is a child who has died, and I get a large number of bereaved parents coming to see me, they cannot understand why a child should have suffered and why a young life has ended. I believe that the length of our lives is preordained at the time we are born. That is what I try to explain to the people who come to see me, but it is particularly hard for them to take on board, especially when there is a child involved. I think we are all date-stamped with the age at which we will die. That may be at two months, two years, twenty years, fifty or eighty years – but the only thing that is certain on the day any of us are born is that we will one day die. The big question is when and I believe that the "when" is preordained.'

Sally says that one thing she has learned is that there is no order or time-scale to grief: 'The textbooks tell people that for the first few months they will feel anger, then they will be sad and then guilty. They say "things will get easier" when the first anniversaries have all passed. But it's not like that at all. A woman came to see me regularly for some time and then stopped. I picked up the phone to her one day, just to see how she was doing. It was, perhaps several years after her husband's death and she told me: "I've had a terrible weekend, Sally. I've just sat on the stairs, howling."

'People might say she should be over it by now. I would like to tell bereaved people that they will never get over death. There will just come a time when they get used to the idea that their loved one is dead and will learn to live with that knowledge. Bereavement is not an illness. The emotions can wash over you like a wave at a sight, a sound, a smell or a touch and the worst thing anyone can say is: "Haven't you got over it yet?" Whatever it is that invokes the wave of despair, that wave is chaotic and has no recognisable pattern to it. That is something that anyone who has been bereaved or who is helping the bereaved needs to understand.'

How does she 'make contact'? 'I don't do tarot or crystals. I just get voices, sometimes in my head, sometimes in my ears,' she says. 'I've had them all my life so I don't know any differently. Yes, there are cranks around, but I believe that rather than damaging genuine psychics, they give us more credibility.'

When people recommend you to a psychic, they will undoubtedly regale you with amazing stories, including the kind of detail that they have no means of knowing. That is what makes the whole question of psychic contact so fascinating. Because, if there is nothing 'there' how can they do it?

Sally Morgan tells the story of how a new client came to see her. She was a young woman and Sally says that as she opened the front door, she was conscious of a little girl dancing round her. It was a spirit child with bobbed blonde hair and she was demanding of Sally: 'I want my hair back. I want my hair. Tell her to give me my hair.'

Sally says that the child was as persistent and as demanding as any small child can be in life. She was, so persistent that she found it hard to greet the woman. At that point, she says, she had no idea why this woman had come to see her and she needed to be very careful what she said. However, the child's voice was so insistent that she found herself saying out loud: 'Wait a minute, darling. You've got your hair. I'll see to you if you wait just a minute,' just as she might have done to a 'live' child.

Eventually, Sally managed to say to the woman: 'Please forgive me if I've got this wrong, and I'm sorry if I upset you, but have you lost a little girl?' The woman said she had. Sally then told her: 'She's got hair. She's got a blonde bob, but she's asking me for her hair.' At this the woman opened her handbag and took out a long, green box. She opened the box and inside was a pony tail tied with a green ribbon.

'I did have a little daughter,' she told Sally. 'She had waist length blonde hair. She was having chemotherapy and she asked me to cut her hair short so that when she lost her hair, she could have a wig made with her own hair. But she died before that could happen.'

Sally advised her to 'give' the child back her hair by burying it near her. 'Some time later, the child's grandfather came to see me,' Sally says. 'He told me that they had had to get permission, but that they had been able to bury the child's hair on her grave, just where the flowers are. I told him I knew that the child was now happy, because she had her hair back.'

Sally says there are times when she can see and hear someone's beloved relative who has died and she worries that the person who is with her is unable to see and hear them too. 'I think if I thought that someone could see or hear my dead child and I couldn't, I would want to tear them apart,' she says. 'Generally, though, people don't think like that at all. They are ecstatic because they know their loved ones are safe and happy. Often they are not with the people their family expect them to be with, but with someone quite unlikely, such as a daughter-in-law with her father-in-law and not her own parents.'

Sally does charity work, giving readings to large gatherings in aid of charity. She agrees that it is as well to be wary of anyone who, in a group situation, asks if there is anyone in the room who knows a 'John' or whether there's a woman here who had a grandma wearing glasses whose name begins with G. There will, of course, always be one – and they will inevitably cling to every word the clairvoyant says without question. 'My contacts come through much more directly,' Sally says. 'I will walk over to someone and say: "You're Olga and your grandmother Mary wants to tell you that you've made a terrible mistake painting that front door pink!" Generally, Olga will be utterly amazed. How could I ever have known about her pink front door? But it's not about proving I'm genuine. I don't need to do that. It's about giving other people hope.'

Lee Van Zahl

Psychic and clairvoyant Lee Van Zahl is a qualified counsellor with a BSc in psychology. She has practised clairvoyance for more than twenty years. She says that as a trained bereavement counsellor who has been lucky enough to be blessed with 'the gift', her counselling training and skills are often called into play.

'I first realised that I was a clairvoyant about three weeks after my own father's death when I was eighteen years old,' she says. 'I was sitting in a chair in my bedroom one night when he came to me and told me, in his own voice, that he was all right. This was not a memory of his voice, ringing in my head. It was the voice he had spoken with all his life and I heard it with my ears, just as though he was in the room.

'Then, one day, I was in the High Street, buying books in preparation for emigrating to the UK when I saw him, quite literally, across the road. He was waving to me and he was wearing his favourite check jacket, a white shirt, black shoes and a nice, maroon colour tie. He was smiling and blowing kisses. It wasn't imagination. It wasn't wishful thinking. He was there.'

Lee sees her work as being 'in the service of people who need me. Sometimes, people don't have strong religious beliefs and after bereavement, they don't know where they are,' she says. 'Without religion, they have no idea which way to go. That's where my work is important. I admit that I do run a business. I have to earn money to pay my rent and most of my work comes from referrals. However, in my work as a clairvoyant, I am not "becoming" the person who has died. I am channelling a signal from that person's life and from their personality and character which is only a little part of what they were in total.

'The responsibility of a psychic is, in my view, enormous. You have to appreciate that someone has made and kept an appointment with you because they don't know where else to turn. During the course of any appointment, if you are unable to bring contact with their loved ones through, you must still address the issues of the bereavement and how it is affecting their everyday life. You need to offer the bereaved person guidelines or insight into themselves so that they can find a reason to get up in the morning.'

Lee advises that before anyone visits a psychic they should be aware that making an appointment with a serious, recognised practitioner should never be done as 'a laugh' or something 'the girls' should get together to do as nothing more than a matter of curiosity.

She suggests you should:

- Ask to see testimonials before you make the appointment. Don't just read them. Check them out by asking if you may telephone or write to one of those whose testimonials you have read.
- DON'T reveal anything about yourself or your dead loved ones before or during the session. Keep quiet and let the clairvoyant do the talking. Don't be terribly disappointed if they don't 'come through'. The one thing no good clairvoyant can do is *make* spirits appear 'to order'.

'I have found that people are becoming much more open to, and interested in, the work of clairvoyants over the past ten to fifteen years,' says Lee. 'They seem able to comprehend that the human being is not just mind and body but that there is something more inside. People seem to be interested in trying to discover their spiritual purpose in life. Often, when someone consults a psychic or clairvoyant, it is not only about death. It is as though they are trying to consult with their own spiritual nature and how they can affect their own spiritual lives.'

Believers – and non-believers

Renee

Renee lost her son Paul in a fatal motorcycle accident more than nineteen years ago. He was seventeen years old. The death was the worst blow she and her husband could ever know. To heap cement blocks of anguish on to their already indescribable pain, his death was followed eighteen months later by the death of her mother, and, a year after that, by the death of a beloved brother. 'My husband and I were both made redundant only eighteen months after Paul was killed,' she says. 'We were devastated and I think when you reach such a low point in your life, you have to go looking for something.

'I was convinced I had to find out where Paul was and what he was doing. I went to a Jewish synagogue and spoke to the Rabbi. I went to see a priest in the Catholic Church and a Church of England vicar. I told all of them I needed to know where Paul was and I think in the end they all got fed up with me. I had heard about Lee Van Zahl, a psychic who had been recommended for her extraordinary talents, but the conventional religious men all said the same thing: "Don't dabble in all that." They advised me to "accept" what had happened, but I couldn't accept it. Everyone grieves differently.'

Renee says that there were three people in her West London street who had all lost children aged between seventeen and twenty-one. 'We'd lost two boys and a girl between us and we all dealt with the situation differently,' she says.

'One mother who lost her daughter to cancer couldn't bear to go into her room after her daughter's death. It was locked and never opened. The lady down the street whose son had died cleared everything out of his room almost straightaway. She couldn't bear to look at it.

'I used to sit in Paul's room and talk. Because I had been made redundant, I had time on my hands. I got in touch with my friend Maureen who had been to a psychic fair. She told me I ought to get in touch with a lady called Lee Van Zahl, a psychic who ran a shop in Stamford Bridge. My husband and I discussed it. We thought nothing ventured, nothing gained. So I made an appointment.'

When Renee went to see Lee, she had a list of urgent questions that she needed to have answered before her mind could rest. 'I needed to know where Paul was, what he was doing and whether he was with my dad,' she says. 'The thought that he might be all alone was very uncomfortable.

'It was a miracle. Everything I needed to know, Lee could tell me. She was able to reassure me that Paul was all right. He was with my dad. He had been surprised to find himself where he was. The accident had been a big shock to him. Of course, anyone could have said the things she said as a way of offering comfort, but then Lee started to tell me things she could never have known. She told me what I had done with his clothes and his bedroom. She told me small details. At first, I wondered whether she was somehow reading my mind. But then, she tells you something really good. She is absolutely brilliant.

'When you have been bereaved, some people prefer you not to mention it. I have had people cross the road rather than face me. They would say that they didn't want to upset me. But you are upset anyway. All I wanted was for them to come over and tell me that they remembered Paul. I wanted him remembered. I didn't want him wiped off the face of the earth. He has been gone now longer than I had him. But thanks to Lee, I feel that he knows I remember him all the time. That's not fantasy. I have been in situations where I think: "Oh God, Paul. Get me out of this." Within five minutes, the phone will ring and the problem will be solved. Lee says there is no such thing as coincidence in such situations. She says there is always a reason. And when songs we played at the funeral blare out from the supermarket tannoy, I know that it is actually Paul who is with me even there and he's saying: "It's all OK, Mum. I am here."

'I may pay Lee for our consultations but I feel that she really cares about me and I know that if I need to speak to her, she's there.'

Angeline

Angeline was devastated after her young husband's sudden and tragic death from a heart attack at the age of just thirty-eight. Fit and healthy, or so she had thought, he was a sports fanatic who jogged daily. There was no warning before he collapsed and died on a tennis court. She struggled on as best she could, fighting to keep her job and cope with three young teenage sons. She couldn't, however, accept her husband's death. 'There was so much unfinished business,' she says. 'There were so many things we hadn't said to one another and so many things we hadn't done together.'

In a shop window near her office, Angeline saw an advert by a man offering his psychic and clairvoyant powers. She didn't know anything about him, but in what she describes as a 'mad moment' she dialled the number on her mobile phone and made an appointment to see him half an hour later.

'I rang the office and told them I wouldn't be back because I had a splitting headache,' she admits. 'I felt something calling me. This was my chance to contact Alan and hear him tell me what he wanted me to do next. I needed his approval for the way I was coping with my life and our children. I was desperate for him to tell me that he was all right. That he still loved me. That he wasn't punishing me by dying. Seeing that card in that window seemed to be my "chance".'

As soon as Angeline walked in she knew she had made a mistake. 'I walked into this tiny office in a very smart office block on London's South Bank,' she says. 'The psychic didn't look particularly savoury. He wasn't tidy or shaven and his fingernails were bitten which put me off.

'Then he held on to one of my hands and told me an elderly man was coming through and he thought it might be my father. As my father was at work in Dartford, I told him I thought that was highly unlikely. Then he told me it must be my grandfather or uncle and asked if I had any relatives called George. I felt he was grasping at straws. I had made up my mind not to reveal anything about myself or my personal circumstances but I'm sure he could tell I was fairly upset and when he said: "I can see you are recently bereaved", I burst into tears and told him about Alan. That was fatal. He went off telling me that everything was fine, Alan was all right and happy and not in pain any more. As he hadn't been in pain at all to my knowledge, that offered me little comfort.

'The psychic told me that Alan wanted "the family" to carry on with all the things we had started – but I know that if Alan had "been there", he would have called the boys by name, or talked about his parents. His mother was absolutely heartbroken and devastated by his death.

During the entire hour I was with the psychic, he didn't say one thing that was remotely pertinent to us or to the lives we had shared together. He didn't get one thing right. I didn't feel he was even particularly sympathetic. I came out feeling I had revealed far too much, had gained precisely nothing, and was £95 poorer into the bargain. I sobbed all the way home on the tube because I felt so let down. I had hoped and prayed to contact Alan and I felt he wasn't there when I needed him most. I'd even felt that if I thought about him hard enough during my session, this psychic would somehow thought-read him from my head. Instead, I'd listened to a load of tripe and I felt worse than when I went in.'

Angeline says she eventually found a good private professional counsellor. 'I pay my counsellor and although sometimes the counselling is hard work, and I do come out feeling sad, at least I know that I'm not dabbling in something I didn't understand and now don't believe in anyway. I just want Alan's soul to rest in peace, wherever it is. I will never dabble in trying to contact him again.'

Malcolm
Although Malcolm, sixty, says that both he and his wife Pam, whom he affectionately calls 'Pammy', knew she was dying, he was still totally devastated by her death a few months ago. 'I can't come to terms with it, even now,' he says.

Malcolm finds it very hard to stay at home alone. 'I walk into the empty house and can't bear not hearing her voice greeting me. So I spend a lot of time with friends. A couple of months ago, I was visiting a friend and just about to go home when we got to talking about psychics. He told me there was this woman across the road who was a well-known psychic and said: "Why don't you go across and see her?" So I went and knocked on the door there and then and Sally welcomed me in. She asked me why I wanted to see a medium and I told her I'd just lost Pammy and I wanted to know if there was any way I could get in touch with her.'

Malcolm says that he was 'taken aback' by the speed at which things progressed. 'She spoke about Pammy as though she knew her,' he says. 'She told me just what kind of warm and caring person she was. She told me she wasn't suffering any more. Although I didn't say a word about him, she also told me that I had lost a grandson. It happened five years ago. I always knew that little Max would be there waiting for Pammy. My daughter-in-law, Max's mother, has always believed in these things. When Max used to go to his other grandparents, he used to like to move things around on the mantelpiece. The little toe-rag still does it. They will wake up in the morning and find things rearranged.

'Anyway, my daughter-in-law came with me on my second visit to Sally. That's when Sally told me that Pammy would eventually come back to the house, that she would be in our home and that I'd see her at a window.

'When I got home, I kept looking at the window, but I couldn't see Pammy. Pammy died on 5 April. On 5 July, I was very tired and went to bed at around 10 p.m. I fell asleep after a while. I was awakened by a noise at about five to twelve. I know the time because I looked at my clock. I called out: "Who's there?" but there was no reply. Then I felt this tremendous pressure on my arm. Like when you have your blood pressure taken. A feeling of tightness. My arm was bulging. All of a sudden, the window in the bedroom lit up completely. The light was so bright that I had to shield my eyes. I have never, ever seen a light like it before. It lasted four or five seconds. Sally had said I would see Pammy, but I didn't see her. Just this light. As the light faded, the pressure on my arm subsided. My hair was standing up on end and I had the feeling that something was running across the bedroom. Then it disappeared.

'I phoned Sally the following day to tell her what had happened. She told me that it was Pam and that she had come back. Pam had been in the bedroom. She told me that next time she came to the house, I would see her and that she would be at the top of the stairs or where water is. That means the bathroom or the kitchen. I'm sure it must be the kitchen. Like all women, Pammy was always in the kitchen.'

Malcolm says he made a promise to his wife that he would never move from the home they shared, and, knowing what Sally has said to him, now he never will. 'The only way I'll leave is the way Pam left, in a coffin,' he says.

'People who have not been through what I've been through don't understand why I'm doing what I'm doing. Every time I go to the cemetery, I speak to other people and they seem to understand how I feel. I can feel Pammy but can't touch her. Part of my life has been taken away from me that I will never, ever be able to replace. When Sally talks to me about Pammy as though she knew her, that brings me a lot of comfort and hope for the future. It is incredible.'

On Malcolm's first visit to Sally, she told him four things in particular and mentioned a couple of names that meant nothing to him. 'But then she suddenly said: "You've got to go and get the umbrella and bring it home." Two days previously, I had been fishing and my umbrella had blown inside out. One or two of the spokes had broken completely and I took it to a shop to be repaired. I know it is a fishing umbrella and it had nothing to do with Pammy, but it was strange. Such a coincidence.' Coincidence? A message from another world?

Laurie Didham of the Child Death Helpline says: 'Scientists have been propounding new theories that we absorb memories and that that is the explanation for some of the strange and inexplicable things that happen,' she says. 'I often catch myself using my father's expressions, as though somehow he is inside my head. It has a fond, warm feeling about it now,' she says. 'Recently, I was on my way back from a holiday in Devon and stopped off at a pub for lunch. Sitting there was a man wearing a woolly cardigan of a kind you rarely see people wear now. My father used to wear cardigans exactly like that and it brought memories of him and lovely warm feelings of him came flooding back.'

Memory, coincidence or something beyond belief? Perhaps we'll never know – until we get wherever our loved ones have gone. But if believing that they are there, 'just around the corner' brings comfort, then you can also believe in Henry Scott Holland's final words in his famous poem: 'All is Well'.

11

Complementary help

Bereavement is the most stressful of all life events. You may not initially *feel* stressed out following bereavement. I can remember a strange kind of calm apparently overwhelming me, indeed so much 'calm' that I could hardly remember where I was or what I was supposed to be doing. It's almost as though you are an 'outsider' looking in on your own life because what is happening isn't actually happening to you, particularly at the beginning. It's happening to your alter ego. But stressed you almost certainly are.

Stress can manifest itself in a host of physical ways: loss of appetite, over-eating, insomnia, lethargy, hyperactivity – these are all significant physical signs of stress, tension and depression.

What is more, bereavement can be as physically demanding as any disease. It exposes stress and disease that may already have been lurking in your being, including the overworked 'muscles' of unrest, mistrust and self-doubt. The physical loss of a loved one is an amputation of a soul closely aligned to your own and needs physical as well as mental readjustment and what may be a period of re-cuperation as exhausting as any you may expect following any other kind of serious surgery. Your self has to learn to survive the loss of another part of self. That may be a parent, partner, child or dearly loved friend, but their presence has been a vital part of your self's existence. And just as people continue to 'feel' amputated limbs, and are sensitive to outside pressures on an arm or leg that is no longer there, so you may experience the sensation of the presence of a loved one you can't see, hear or feel except in your head.

Doctors may prescribe antidepressants or sedatives as prostheses to help you through the process of grieving. Take them when they're offered, if you think they will help. There's no shame in accepting all the assistance that you can get. However, there are also many complementary therapies that may be able to give you an extra 'lift', and I think it's worth trying anything to make you feel better as you fight to come to terms with what has happened.

Complementary therapies such as aromatherapy, meditation and yoga, reflexology, homoeopathy and herbalism have been around for thousands of years. There are sceptics who say their benefits are 'all in the mind' because they are mostly scientifically 'unproven'. The problem is that it would cost drug companies literally millions of pounds to run clinical trials to test their efficacy – money these companies are loathe to part with. You have nothing to lose and everything to gain by trying them. They will give you 'space' for yourself you might not otherwise make, with time to clear your mind and relax your body. Such relaxation of body and spirit can only serve to create a stronger physical you. And on the bottom line there is only one person who can help you learn to live with what has happened and become comfortable again – and that is you yourself. Picking up the shattered pieces of life following bereavement is never easy but anything that helps must be worth a try. Don't do it for anyone else's sake. Do it for your own.

Aromatherapy

Massage has been practised as a soothing therapy for thousands of years. The Romans loved their scented oils but, as a treatment in its own right, aromatherapy has only risen to prominence during the last two decades. When another person works with tender, firm and caring hands on your battered and forlorn-feeling being, it can literally soothe your soul. Add to that the wonderful scents of herbs and spices, which have long been known to bring a sense of comfort and balmy relief to a troubled spirit, and you have aromatherapy.

Angela Warren, a qualified aromatherapist masseuse and stress counsellor at the Nuffield Hospital in Exeter, says she often uses her skills as an aromatherapist to help people work through the process of grieving.

'Obviously, every case is individual and I try to listen and hear what stage a grieving person is at before recommending the essential oils I feel will help them best,' she says. 'I generally use a blend of three oils at any one time, according to the needs of the bereaved person.'

Angela finds that:

Rose oils help overcome initial anger at what has happened because they 'soften' the grief and allow it to come out and ease the pain.

Frankincense calms and clears the mind, bringing a feeling of tranquillity. It also works on the lungs which tend to 'hold' grief.

Citrus oils are also very good at helping release anger, and work against the negativity of grief, giving people an uplift and helping them see the future more positively.

Camomile will help relieve stress and tension and feelings of helplessness and vulnerability and will alleviate insomnia.

Lavender used in conjunction with camomile will almost certainly help build up the immune system, which will have taken a severe knock. Lavender can be quite comforting and nurturing.

Marjoram may help combat feelings of loneliness and aloneness when you are feeling cut-off from the rest of the world by reason of your bereavement.

Benison is not used often but is a lovely warming oil which gives the feeling of being held. It has a lovely sweet vanilla smell.

Cyprus is another oil traditionally used to combat grief. If you are stuck in a rut of grief, it can help you to move forward and let go of what has happened. It also opens the lungs in a similar way to frankincense, and brings strength to the whole body and mind.

'The experience of a massage will help bring your body to your own attention. It will calm the nervous system and bring you "into the moment" which is where you need to be,' Angela says. 'It will help improve circulation, relax muscles and hopefully persuade you to see things in a different perspective.

'As a stress counsellor, I know that when someone is feeling vulnerable and helpless, the important thing is to help him or her find time and space for themselves. A masseuse is someone who will be giving you attention on a "one-to-one" basis, caring about what is happening to you. At a time when you may be feeling abandoned and very lonely, it is important to feel cherished, even if only for just an hour or so.'

Although an aromatherapy massage may be the perfect solution, restraints of time or money or a combination of both may make it impractical, particularly in the early stages of bereavement. However, this does not mean that because you can't get to an aromatherapy masseuse, you can't take full advantage of the benefits essential oils offer.

Although an aromatherapy massage may last between an hour and an hour and a quarter, and can be a great investment, massaging yourself with relevant essential oils or adding aromatherapy preparations to your bath can have very beneficial effects.

Boots and The Body Shop now offer an extensive range of aromatherapy preparations which you can add to your toilette at a very reasonable cost.

Oriental medicine

Chinese and Japanese medical practices date back many thousands of years. Both are based on the belief that the thought processes and mental orientation of every one of us are directly connected with the organs of the body.

John Brazier, a director of the Academy of Oriental Medicine, explains how this has a bearing on the help that Oriental medical practitioners can offer those who have been bereaved:

'When a person has suffered a bereavement, we believe their

mental state has a physical impact on their body,' he says. 'Bereavement often leads to depression. When someone is suffering from the depression occasioned by bereavement, often their livers and spleens don't work as effectively as they should. They will often lose their appetites because their stomachs are literally churning over. They will be having loose bowel movements. This is a direct physical reaction to mental stimuli, proving that the body and mind are one.

'You can spot a depressed person across a road. Their shoulders will be stooped. Their back and head bent. Their eyes will be looking towards the ground. You can see their mental condition from their body language. If the body is not in strong working order, any trauma will cause a fairly dramatic mental reaction. We work by connecting the anger, anxieties, fears and irritations, the mental symptoms to the parts of the body they relate to addressing "treatments" to those body parts. Oriental medical practitioners believe they can help restore the physical and mental status quo.'

Chinese medical practitioners believe that:

- The spleen is highly related to anxious states of the mind.
- Kidneys are related to fear and fright.
- The liver is related to anger and irritation.
- The lungs are related to grief.

'When you go to a funeral, you will see people reacting in very different ways to their loss,' John Brazier continues. 'This is not only due to the relationship they had with the deceased, but also how physically well and fit the body was before the bereavement and the physical health pre-bereavement will determine the way an individual will cope with the stress of loss.'

Oriental medical practitioners often treat depression with *acupuncture*, the placing of fine needles along energy lines known as meridians to help redress the balance of the body. They will also use massage at *acupressure* points as well as using *herbal treatments*.

Homoeopathy

Homoeopathy is a system of medicine based upon the principle of treating like with like. The theory is that if the medication prescribed to treat a set of symptoms were to be given in large doses, it would produce the symptoms the patient is complaining of. The medicines prescribed by homoeopathic practitioners are made from natural ingredients such as plant extracts, diluted a hundredfold.

Many homoeopathic doctors are also conventionally qualified medical practitioners who have undertaken postgraduate medical studies in homoeopathy. However, not all homoeopathic practitioners have studied conventional medicine.

Raj Baines, Registrar for the Homoeopathic Medical Association, explains: 'Of course, there can be no "treatment" for bereavement, but homoeopathy looks at treating a "whole" person rather than a set of symptoms. The beauty of homoeopathic remedies is that they are easily available, offer relief from symptoms within just a few days and are non-addictive or habit-forming as conventional prescription drugs may be. Homoeopathic doctors take the mind as the most important "symptom" because this obviously relates to the individual more than physical symptoms do.'

Homoeopathic practitioner and author Beth MacEoin says that bereavement, like divorce, signals the end of a relationship. She says she believes that many 'over-the-counter' remedies can bring immediate relief to someone who has been bereaved, especially in the early stages. 'If they do not prove effective enough, it is always sensible to contact a homoeopathic practitioner who may be able to offer individual help based on personal need and diagnosis,' she says.

As homoeopathic remedies do not have side-effects as many conventional antidepressants do, and are not habit forming, it is easy to switch from one to the other quite painlessly. 'When someone who is self-treating realises they are responding positively to a remedy, that is the time to stop taking it,' says Beth MacEoin. 'They do not need to wean themselves off one drug before embarking on another. On the other hand, positive feelings are a sign that the whole system has responded well and the patient should continue to improve even after they have stopped taking the remedy.

'If, on the other hand, there is no sign of a positive reaction, they should go on to take another course of the treatment. Homoeopathic remedies help someone work through the natural process that they need to go through in the initial stages of grief. If they are unable to work through this process, they may have the unpleasant experience of getting stuck in a mire of grieving and being unable to move on.'

Beth MacEoin recommends the following 'over-the-counter' remedies for instant self-help after bereavement:

Ignatia

This can be taken in the very early stages after experiencing bereavement. It is very beneficial in the days between the death and the funeral. It will help people who have involuntary bouts of weeping (which, Beth MacEoin says, are absolutely natural and normal although they can in themselves be quite distressing). The weeping itself can be so wearing that it can bring them to the point of feeling it is all too much to bear. Ignatia can be very helpful in helping someone come to terms with the shock of bereavement. It will also help soothe churning digestive systems.

Natrum mur

This helps when someone feels their emotions have been 'suspended'; although they feel they want to cry, they are always on the brink of tears, but the tears won't flow. Natrum mur is very beneficial when someone presents a picture of withdrawal. Emotionally, they withdraw from socialising, particularly from company that is known to be very warm, affectionate and sympathetic. When people move into this state, they may find it very uncomfortable to be in receipt of affection. It is almost as though if they break down in such company, they will find it humiliating.

Some of the physical symptoms indicating that natrum mur will be helpful include:

- Recurrent colds, specifically those associated with cold sores.
- Irregular eating habits and a craving for salty foods because of the strong taste.

Because natrum mur has a close relationship with ignatia, when someone has done well with ignatia, they will benefit greatly from natrum mur when they move on.

Pulsatilla

This is the exact opposite to natrum mur. It is especially helpful for people who actively seek out sympathetic company. It helps those who have a tremendous sense of release after having a good cry on a sympathetic shoulder. Someone taking pulsatilla may also benefit enormously from gentle exercise such as going for a walk in the fresh air. It is worth considering if someone has a disturbed sleeping pattern following bereavement. It will also help with other symptoms such as recurrent headaches, and severe indigestion as a result of feeling stressed which is obviously aggravated by eating fatty foods. Pulsatilla will also offer some relief if a woman is suffering symptoms which become worse pre-menstrually.

Both practitioners recommend phosphoric acid to treat feelings of indifference, disinterest in the world around one, and lack of motivation.

If you are in any doubt about a practitioner's qualifications, you can consult the register at the Faculty of Homoeopathic Medicine at the Royal London Homoeopathic Hospital or find a consultant through the Homoeopathic Medical Association at 6 Livingstone Road, Gravesend, Kent DA12 5DZ (tel: 01474 560 336). Or you can contact the Society of Homoeopaths on 01604 621 400. You do not need a referral to visit a homoeopathic practitioner.

Herbalism

Herbalism is the treatment of people with plants, parts of plants, or plant extracts. Herbalists believe that depression caused by bereavement can be successfully helped by herbal remedies including wild oats, lemon balm, ginseng, wood betony, basil and St John's Wort, the only herbal remedy which has scientific testing and received conventional medical approval. However, St John's Wort should be treated with great respect.

Dr Donald Brown of Bastyr University in Seattle recommends that people with fair skins should avoid exposure to strong sunlight and other sources of ultraviolet light when taking St John's Wort because of cases of photosensitivity which have been reported. He also advises avoiding foods that contain tyramine, alcoholic drinks and certain medications such as tyrosine, narcotics, amphetamines, and over-the-counter cold and flu remedies while taking St John's Wort. Furthermore, this is a herbal drug that should never be taken in conjunction with prescription antidepressants. It is also Dr Brown's opinion that St John's Wort should not be used by a pregnant woman or by a mother who is breastfeeding. Nor should it be taken with warferin. Before taking St John's Wort, and if you are taking any other prescription medicines, it is essential to consult your doctor.

The aim of herbalism is to help the body help itself, so that harmony and balance may be restored and healing may take place. Herbal medicines are said to work biochemically, triggering neurochemical responses in the body. Taken in moderate doses for long enough, these biochemical responses become automatic, even after one stops taking the herbs. Herbal formulas have three basic functions:

- Elimination and detoxification: herbs are used as diuretics, laxatives and blood purifiers – one step in healing.
- Health management and maintenance: herbs are used to counter-act physical symptoms and stimulate the body's own self-healing powers.
- Health building: herbs are used to tone the organs and nourish the tissues and blood.

Mr Ray Hill, Secretary of the British Herbal Medicine Association says: 'St John's Wort will certainly help mild to medium depression.

Kava kava can be taken where there is significant anxiety. Bach Flower Remedies really work on the emotional level, which is where the problems with bereavement lie. Anyone who needs help can get in touch with us here and we will recommend a herbal practitioner. The British Herbal Medicine Association can be found at Sun House, Church Street, Stroud, Glos. GL5 1JL (tel: 01453 751389).

Herbal medicine is balanced in its constituents and is safe when prescribed by a herbal practitioner. Side effects are rare and effects are usually not cumulative. Medicines are made from any part of a plant and from any plant that has chemical constituents of medicinal value. This means that a herb may be a tree or a weed.

Herbal medicine is usually taken in tincture form (which is an alcoholic extract), pill or powder form, or in a tea (infusion) or brew (decoction). In some countries it is even taken in soup. It has to be taken regularly and consistently to achieve results. The herbalist usually gives dietary and nutritional advice to complement the treatment. Herbalism is quite different from homoeopathy in that the medication is not diluted and shaken. Nor is medicine matched up to personality types as in homoeopathy. Herbal medicine works more on the physiological systems directly rather than on energy levels. This means that is fast and effective if chosen correctly.

Bach Flower Remedies

If you are recently bereaved and have been under great stress, you have no doubt already been offered Bach's Rescue Remedy.

I have to admit that I must have been living on another planet until my own bereavements because I had actually never heard of Bach's Flower Remedies before. Somebody put a few drops of the Rescue Remedy on my tongue just prior to the funerals and whether the effect was psychological or physiological, I felt more eased.

I now know better. Bach Flower Remedies are another form of herbalism, easily obtained from chemists almost everywhere. Dr Bach was an eminent physician whose medical experience and expertise was highly regarded in the early twentieth century. He was deeply involved in both homoeopathy and immunology but his great life's work was the discovery of thirty-eight flower remedies, which he aligned to different moods and emotions. He believed that the actions of these remedies could restore the balance between mind, body and spirit by helping the sufferer overcome negative attitudes such as worry, hopelessness and irritability and which, he believed, were so often the cause of ill-health. The Bach Remedies do not claim to treat physical disease, but they do claim that by bringing about a state of mind that is conducive to health and happiness, one's whole system has a chance to respond positively and begin its own natural healing process.

According to Stefan Ball, author of *Teach Yourself Bach Flower Remedies*, who works at Bach's base at Mount Vernon near Wallingford in Oxfordshire (where Dr Bach spent the final two years of his life), the remedies most likely to help those suffering from bereavement include:

- Sweet chestnut – which will help alleviate the extreme anguish the bereaved may experience when they feel there is no point going on with life. It purports to lift the gloom surrounding the grieving person and to help them 'let go' so that they can move forward again with at least some measure of hope and expectation.
- Star of Bethlehem – to be used to help minimise the effects of the shock of bereavement. Star of Bethlehem is often the first remedy offered after bereavement because it is believed to help overcome the numbness that people commonly feel, so that the grieving process itself, an essential part of healing, can begin sooner. Dr Bach called it the 'comforter of pain and sorrow'.
- Pine remedy – is best for those who may feel guilty and believe they could or should have done more, once they have recovered from the initial shock and despair following a death. There comes a time when these initial reactions are replaced or compounded by other emotions – including guilt, the tendency to live too much in the past, resentment or doubts about one's ability to cope with everyday responsibilities – and pine is helpful for people who find themselves in this situation.

- Willow remedy – is recommended as a therapy for self-pity, anger and frustration. It is billed as the opposite of pine, of use to people who want to blame someone else for what has happened, instead of taking responsibility for the death upon themselves. This is for the person who, rather than talking of lost happiness, grumbles about the present and how hard life is now as a result of the death. It is for people who would expect others to share their misery. It is believed to help the person to move forward in a clearer frame of mind and to slowly begin to discover the joy in their own life, as well as rejoicing in other people's.

- Honeysuckle remedy – is also for those who become introspective. It can help those who turn the natural tendency to reminisce about the pleasant times spent in the company of the loved one into morbid and excessive grieving where the mourner lives in the past and has no mind to the present or the future. 'Honeysuckle remedy will lead the attention back to the present so that the grief can be lived through now, experienced and allowed to fade naturally,' says Stefan Ball.

- Elm remedy – can help overcome feelings of helplessness, especially for those who find themselves alone for the first time and faced with coping with everyday tasks once performed by a lost partner. For example, the elm may offer a lift to a woman faced with dealing with financial affairs or coping with a large garden alone, while a man faced with housekeeping chores he has never undertaken before may find elm remedy gives him the confidence he is lacking.

Leaflets on Bach Flower Remedies are available at most leading chemists or may be obtained by writing directly to The Dr Edward Bach Centre, Mount Vernon, Sotwell, Oxfordshire OX10 0PZ. Telephone the Centre on 01491 834678 or visit their website at www.bachcentre.com.

Reflexology

Originating in China where it has been used for thousands of years, reflexology is a relaxation therapy using a form of massage on small areas, or 'reflex points', on the feet.

It is based on the belief that each part of the foot corresponds to a specific part of the body. When we are stressed, such as at times of bereavement or after illness, reflexologists believe that the body is in a state of 'imbalance'. They believe that sensitive areas in the feet indicate which part of the body is congested. Reflexology is recommended as a way of calming yourself, whether you are stressed or going into a stressful situation.

Reflexology was introduced into Britain in 1960 by Doreen Bayly who founded the Bayly Training School for Reflexologists. This is now run by Nicola Hall who took over as the school's Director in 1980 and is the teaching body of the British Reflexologists' Association.

'It is possible to treat the whole body through the feet using reflexology,' says Nicola Hall. 'It is a holistic therapy in that it will treat the whole person, so it works not only on the physical level but on the emotional, and perhaps even spiritual, level as well. It can be used to treat physical conditions as well as purely for relaxation.'

Nicola Hall says that when someone is suffering from stress after bereavement, the stress will manifest physically by attacking their weakest physical points. Some may find they suffer from headaches or irritable bowel while others may suffer skin rashes. The treatment is aimed at both the person's physical and mental state.

Nicola Hall explains that every part of our feet corresponds to areas in the rest of the body. For example, a chart issued by the Bayly school shows:

- The big toe – relates to head and brain. Includes reflexes to the pituitary and pineal glands.
- The first toe – relates to sinuses, which may be sore and irritated following uncontrolled crying.
- The footpad beneath first and second toe – relates to the eyes.

- A small area to the edge of the foot beneath the small toe – relates to the shoulders, which may be extremely tense and taut after bereavement.
- The area beneath the ball of the foot – relates to the stomach and a small patch, centre-foot beneath the area representing the stomach is aligned to the gall bladder.
- A band across the heel – corresponds to the sciatic nerve.

Another reflexology practitioner and lecturer, Avril Nova, says: 'When we are doing a treatment we are actually dealing with internal body energy. Electrical energy comes from the nervous system and chemical energy from the endocrine system, which is the part of our bodies which produces the hormones.

'When you have bereavement, you are emotionally upset and the first place affected by emotional upset is the endocrine system. This can have an effect on the whole nervous system making the person feel very low. Scientific research has shown that the DNA of a cell physically changes when a person is suffering bereavement and that is the reason that the immune system is so susceptible. This is why we see that every human cell in the body can be affected when people are very emotionally upset, such as at times of bereavement and this in turn leads to physical symptoms.'

This is just a brief outline of what reflexology is about. Reflexology is a serious science and only a qualified practitioner is able to diagnose the energy imbalance, showing whether there could be physical or emotional congestion in the corresponding areas.

'When receiving reflexology treatment, every single nerve and pathway will receive stimulation from the therapist so that the body is treated as a whole,' says Nicola Hall. 'Reflex areas which appear tender, indicate an imbalance, and those specifically related to the conditions present will receive extra massage. Treatment sessions generally last about an hour. Sometimes, there may be reactions as the body strives to remove toxins from the system but they will soon pass, leaving the patient feeling relieved and less stressed.'

Yoga

Vi Neale-Smith, General Secretary of the British Wheel of Yoga, was herself bereaved sixteen years ago. She says that yoga helped her in more ways than one.

'The word "yoga" means "union",' she explains. 'It is meant to be a conscious union of your body, your mind and your breath so that whatever you do, the key to it all is the breathing. That is based on very good research. The way you breathe very strongly influences everything else. People who are depressed slump so there is pressure on the front of their bodies, their chests are not open so they are not breathing properly. Their breathing becomes depressed and shallow. And this is where the postures of yoga come in. The way you hold your body is important to the way you feel. If you are breathing properly and calmly, you can't feel agitated in your mind. In most yoga classes, you will find that, however simple the movements, even if you are just raising your arms above your head, you would do it on an 'in' breath and you breathe out as you lower your arms. This is just a starting point to control your movement by the way you control your breath. Control is the operative word. Learning to control your breathing means learning to control your body and through your body, your mind. Having a quiet mind can bring you peace, and by finding peace of mind you may be able to let go. Even your sleeping patterns will improve.'

Vi says that yoga is a very profound subject. 'The path to yoga is paved with good books,' she smiles. 'There are so many on the market that making a single recommendation is hard. Look for a book that contains some breathing exercises and explains about concentration. The whole point of yoga is to be able to meditate, although yoga has no religious connotations at all. It is just a means of finding quietness.'

According to Vi, the pranic network on which yoga exercises are based corresponds approximately to the energy meridians acknowledged in acupuncture, reflexology, shiatsu and all the other healing techniques.

Of course, the best way to practise yoga or any other alternative therpay is under the guidance of a trained expert. Yoga classes, like any other form of relaxation, have much to offer not only in the practise of the therapy themselves but as a means of social contact to those who are bereaved, bereft and feeling isolated. Joining a yoga class may be a means to reconnecting with others.

However, where joining a class is not possible, the exercises themselves can stand alone as a way to relax and rediscover yourself as a whole person. If you can't find a class, or can't find the time to get to one, here are a series of simple exercises to try at home:

- Choose a well-ventilated room in which to practise; it should be somewhere where you won't be interrupted.
- Wear loose clothing, i.e. loose-fitting trousers and a shirt or T-shirt.
- Avoid wearing anything restrictive such as belts or waistbands.
- It is not a good idea to do yoga on a full stomach, so do not eat at least three hours before you practise yoga or go to a class, or half an hour after a class. This prevents cramp and other feelings of discomfort.
- If you have a serious medical condition, spinal problems or flu, ensure you have your GP's approval before deciding to practise yoga.

Complete breathing

This is breathing in the complete way. Best practised first thing as you get up, before breakfast, or before retiring to bed. Rest your palms on your stomach and exhale to empty your lungs. Inhale slowly, sliding your hands upwards while your diaphragm moves down. Your lungs fill with fresh air. When it feels natural to breathe out, exhale while sliding your hands down your stomach, expelling all the stale air from the lungs. Repeat this four times.

Meridian exercises:

The meridian exercises can be practised daily – if possible, at the same regular times in the morning or before you go to sleep.

They are the ideal precursor to the full postures, especially if you are having any particular stiffness or problems with mobility of the joints. They may seem very simple, but have a profound effect with regular practice.

Yoga postures

Please remember you do these exercises at your own risk. Proceed carefully and with respect for your own body and its limitations.

The meridian exercises can be performed by anyone with normal physical mobility. They take ten minutes to perform and can be done once or twice a day. Regular daily practice is most effective.

These rotation and bending exercises exercise all the joints, fingers and toes. They are easy to perform and help maintain and balance the flow of subtle energy through the body and so prevent the onset of disease and increase the sense of vitality.

They can also help the body and mind build up resistance to disease.

Five rotations each way, or five bends, should be enough on each exercise, unless you feel resistance, pain, or energy blockages which need more repetitions to clear. It can help to fix your mind on some kind of positive image or theme, or even think of the yogis who have developed this form of health.

First of all, rotate fingers, toes, hips and shoulders clockwise. For reference as to which way this is, with the thumb, for instance, one uses an imaginary clock at the base of the thumb facing outwards towards the tip of the thumb.

1. SITTING on the floor with legs straight out in front:

a) FINGER ROTATIONS – start by taking the outstretched left thumb in the right hand and rotate it five times clockwise and five times anti-clockwise, using as your reference the imaginary clock facing upwards from the base of the thumb. Take each finger in turn and rotate each way five times, starting with the first finger and ending with the small finger.

b) FINGER SQUEEZING – squeeze the base of each finger in turn, starting with the thumb, and clear off any stagnant subtle energy by sliding the fingers along it to the tip with some pressure.

Now perform similar rotations, squeezing on the right hand, starting with the thumb, and working down the fingers to the little finger.

c) TOE ROTATIONS – place the right ankle on the left thigh and, starting with the big toe, rotate each toe five times, clockwise and then anti-clockwise, using the base of the toe as a reference for the direction of rotation.

d) ALTERNATE TOE BENDING – bend the toes, two at a time, in opposite directions back and forth, working along from the big and second toe towards the fourth and little toe.

e) TOE SQUEEZING – gently slide the fingers along from the base of each toe and clear any stagnant energy, sliding the finger and thumb off each toe to stimulate the flow of chi, i.e. energy.

f) FOOT MASSAGE – work down from the top of the foot at least three times with the thumbs of both hands, working out any points of tension or pain. One can refer to a map of the foot and make a mental note of the particular correlation to the whole body of any area of pain or tension, be it the spine or the stomach or eyesight. One can extend the area of massage to the harder sides and topsides of the foot and also work out any tension around the heel.

To clear any blocked energy, one can gently thump the sole of the foot a few times with a loose fist.

Repeat rotations, bending, squeezing and foot massage on left foot, having stretched right foot out in front of yourself.

2) TOE BENDING – with both feet together, bend the toes five times, curling the toes towards the floor and back to you.

3) ANKLE BENDING – curl your toes and point both feet towards the floor five times – this uses the whole foot and ankle, unlike toe bending which is confined to the toes.

4) ROTATING FOOT TO EASE ANKLE – feet thirty centimetres apart, rotate right foot five times each way, then repeat

with left. Then bring feet together and rotate both together five times each way. Describe a circle in the air with the big toes to keep the feet under control.

5) ANKLE CRANKING – place the right ankle on the left thigh and grasp the ankle in the right hand and rotate the foot with the left hand. Five times clockwise and anti-clockwise. Repeat with left foot on right thigh.

6) KNEE BENDING – bend leg and join hands just above the knee joint. Extend and retract the foot to bend the knee, five times right side, then left.

7) HALF-BUTTERFLY HIP BEND – take the right foot in the left hand and use the right hand on the knee to bend the hip joint five times, bringing it up towards the chest and down towards the floor, but without forcing it. Repeat on left leg.

8) HIP JOINT ROTATION – take the right foot in the left hand again and use the right hand on the knee to rotate the hip joint five times clockwise, then anti-clockwise. Repeat on the left leg.

9) FULL BUTTERFLY – press the feet together so the soles and toes meet and stretch inner thigh. Lean forward to stretch spine.

10 & 11) HAND STRETCHING AND CLENCHING – stretch and clench hands, forming a fist with thumb inside, both hands together, five times.

12) WRIST BENDING – hands out in front of you, palms down. Flip the hand up and down to stretch the wrists. Both hands together, five times.

13) WRIST ROTATION – rotate clenched fist to clear flow of energy through wrists, right hand first, then left, then together. Clockwise, then anti-clockwise. Five times each way.

14) ELBOW BENDING – extend arms out in front with palms to the ceiling. Bend elbows by bringing the finger tips to shoulders. Repeat five times. Now stretch out arms to the sides with palms still facing upwards and touch the shoulders with finger tips five times together to bend elbows again.

15) SHOULDER ROTATION – keep the finger tips on the shoulders and elbows out to the side and rotate both together five times clockwise, five times anti-clockwise, to free up the shoulders.

16) NECK ROTATION – gently rotate the head three times clockwise and back again, anti-clockwise, to release any tension in the neck.

17) MOUNTAIN POSE OR TADASANA – strand straight with feet and heels and toes together, tail bone tucked in, stretch hands above head with palms together.

'All is Well'

Death is nothing at all. I have only slipped away into the next room. I am I and you are you. Whatever we were to each other, that we still are. Call me by my old familiar name, speak to me in the easy way that you always used. Put no difference in your tone, wear no forced air of solemnity or sorrow. Laugh as we always laughed at the little jokes we enjoyed together. Play, smile, think of me, pray for me. Let my name be ever the household word that it always was, let it be spoken without effect, without the trace of a shadow on it. Life means all that it ever meant. It is the same as it ever was; there is unbroken continuity. Why should I be out of mind because I am out of sight? I am waiting for you, for an interval, somewhere very near, just round the corner.

All is well.

Henry Scott Holland (1847–1918)
Canon of St Paul's Cathedral

Further reading

Rebecca Abrams and Dora Black, *When Parents Die* (Routledge).

Stefan Ball, *Teach Yourself Bach Flower Remedies* (Hodder & Stoughton).

Shmuley Boteach, *Why Can't I Fall in Love* (Hodder & Stoughton).

Donna Dickenson, Malcolm Johnson and Jeanne Samson Katz (editors), *Death, Dying and Bereavement* (Sage Publications).

Paul Elmshurst (editor), *Wills and Probate* (Which Books).

Virginia Ironside, *You'll Get Over It* (Penguin).

C.S. Lewis, *A Grief Observed* (HarperCollins).

Anne McCracken and Mary Semel (editors), *A Broken Heart Still Beats: After your child dies* (Hazelden Education and Information Services).

Rabbi Julia Neuberger, *Dying Well* (Radcliffe Medical Press).

Harriet Sarnoff Schiff, *The Bereaved Parent* (Souvenir Press).

James Van Praagh, *Healing Grief* (Piatkus).

Alison Wertheimer, *A Special Scar* (Routledge).

Rabbi Jonathan Wittenberg, *The Laws of Life – A guide to traditional Jewish practice at times of bereavement* (The Assembly of Masorti Synagogues, 10978 Finchley Road, London NW11 0PU).

Susan J. Zonnabelt-Smeenge and Robert C. De Vries, *The Empty Chair – Handling grief on holidays and special occasions* (Baker House Books).

In addition, the Child Bereavement Trust has produced two books, *Grieving After the Death of Your Baby* and *Teenage Guide to Coping with Bereavement*, and a video, *When Our Baby Died*.

Index